PRAISE FOR
FROM BURNOUT TO PURPOSE

"From *Burnout to Purpose* explores what's common among those who are successful, happy and fulfilled by their work, and what is common among those who experience the exact opposite. If you struggle in a job that's draining your energy and spirit, or if you feel like you're destined for burnout, this book will help you pivot to purpose."

—SHAWN ACHOR,
The *New York Times* bestselling author of
The Happiness Advantage and *Big Potential*

"I recommend *From Burnout to Purpose* for anyone who wants to learn how to achieve a sense of purpose and fulfillment—especially while working for someone else. That's typically talked about only in entrepreneurship."

—ELLEN ROGIN,
The *New York Times* bestselling author
of *Picture Your Prosperity*

"Do you wonder *How on Earth did I get so burned out? How did this happen … to ME?!* From Burnout to Purpose has unique answers to that question and offers you a path back to power, purpose, and peace for your work."

—JANET BRAY ATTWOOD,
co-author of The *New York Times* bestsellers
The Passion Test and *Your Hidden Riches*

"If you used to be happy with your work, but now you're feeling burned out or questioning if you're on the right path, *From Burnout to Purpose* can show how you may have taken a wrong turn. *From Burnout to Purpose* offers powerful solutions for getting back on track to loving your work."

—MARCI SHIMOFF,
#1 *New York Times* bestselling author, *Happy for No Reason* and
Chicken Soup for the Woman's Soul

"What if everything you learned about achieving career happiness and success was missing a key ingredient? *From Burnout to Purpose* takes the concepts of self-care, well-being, and connecting with a sense of purpose to a new level. It's an accessible approach for taking your power back, aligning with fulfillment, and recovering from feeling depleted at the deepest level."

—CHRIS ATTWOOD,
co-author of The *New York Times* bestsellers
The Passion Test and *Your Hidden Riches*

FROM
BURNOUT
TO
PURPOSE

FROM
BURNOUT
TO
PURPOSE

Simple Strategies for
a Soul-Fulfilling Approach to Work

GINA S. CALVANO

FROM BURNOUT TO PURPOSE
Simple Strategies for a Soul-Fulfilling Approach to Work

Copyright © 2022 Gina S. Calvano

Production & Publishing Consultant: AuthorPreneur Publishing Inc.—geoffaffleck.com
Editor: Nina Shoroplova—ninashoroplova.ca
Proofreader: Lisa Turner—turnercreekpublishing.com
Cover Designer: pagatana.com
Interior Designer: Amit Dey—amitdey2528@gmail.com
Author headshots: Art by Corie

ISBN: 978-1-7373872-0-6 (paperback)
ISBN: 978-1-7373872-1-3 (eBook)
ISBN: 978-1-7373872-2-0 (audiobook)

Library of Congress Number: 2021913664

BUS012000 BUSINESS & ECONOMICS / Careers / General
OCC019000 BODY, MIND & SPIRIT / Inspiration & Personal Growth
SEL024000 SELF-HELP / Self-Management / Stress Management

GIVE YOURSELF THE BEST OPPORTUNITY POSSIBLE TO GET THE MOST OUT OF THIS BOOK!

Download the *From Burnout to Purpose Workbook*

This companion guide is a practical tool to help make learning and practicing the concepts in this book as easy as possible. It includes a chapter-by-chapter recap—a summary of all the key concepts alongside your personal notes so you can refresh your mind right when you need it.

Access your copy at fromburnouttopurpose.com

If we can change some of the external conditions at the work-place that contribute to our dissatisfaction, we certainly should. If not, although it is not always easy or quick, it is still possible to be happy at work through reshaping our attitudes and outlook, through inner training.

His Holiness, the Dalai Lama

CONTENTS

NOTE TO THE READER

I am a career coach and former head of a human resources department. I cultivated my understanding of how we do powerful work we love—despite being in a job we may hate—over nearly thirty years. In that time I have listened, learned, taught, coached, counseled, and applied in my own life and career what I have witnessed from both star and less-than-engaged performers. The stories and perspective I share in this book are my experiences and observations. I include details I believe are most relevant to the points I am teaching. I've done my best to portray my perspective and impressions while protecting the identity of those who have taught me along my path so that I could one day share with you a way to shift to your path of purpose.

Please know, and keep in mind, that I am not a licensed physician or a mental health professional, nor am I ordained in any spiritual vocation. I am simply a dedicated student of self-discovery and an observant servant and guide seeking to share what I have learned, experienced, and witnessed in myself and others over my life so far. It is with gratitude and joy that I offer tools, coaching, approaches, and strategies to enable a workforce that lives and works more consciously from a connected sense of purpose and feels destined for success.

I do not intend, nor should you construe, that I am giving you individual advice. Nor am I dispensing medical, legal, therapeutic, psychological, or spiritual methodologies or advice. This book is not to be used as a substitute for medical treatment, psychotherapy, or another health program of any nature, regardless of what you may believe or have heard from anyone. I do not prescribe the use of any technique in this book as a form of treatment for physical, emotional, or medical problems. Should you require or already be under the care of a physician or mental health professional, seek their advice in this matter.

My only intent is to share personal observations, experiences, strategies, approaches, and techniques that I have observed help people. This book was created to offer you a way to discover and create new possibilities for being more effective in realizing your own personal and career-related well-being, to enhance your self-awareness, soul care, and choice-making skills. This book is not about what the organization you work for can do for you. Rather, it's about what you can do for yourself to prevent and heal from the dimensions of job burnout.

We all face moments of challenge and success in our careers. A major purpose of this book is self-discovery—to help you learn the subtle art of self-observation—so that you can recognize and nurture yourself through experiences that might have you on the path to burnout. Should you observe yourself on that path, my wish is for you to apply what you learn from this book to yourself and to feel equipped to make new choices that enable you to pivot onto a path of purpose.

In choosing to read this book and apply its ideas, advice, and strategies, you embrace that you are responsible for your own success, failure, and risks associated with making new life and career choices. You own your life and the choices you make, despite known or unknown external factors such as the economy, employers, and what other people do or say. In that, neither I nor the people who helped me produce this book own the outcomes—good or bad—that you may experience from practicing what is shared in this book. I wish you clarity, confidence, and conviction for your life and work.

Gina Calvano
Morristown, NJ

PRELUDE TO PURPOSE

Are You Feeling Burned Out—I Can Relate

Does your job have you feeling burned out? Very early in my career, mine did. Yet when I was in my early twenties, I didn't call what I did in response to that feeling as "choosing a path of purpose." I just remembered making a conscious decision to have "a good life"—whatever that meant. I wish I had known the power of that decision at the time I made it. I would have made that decision long before becoming burned out by the age of twenty-six.

It's true, by twenty-six years of age I was burned out.

However, you never would have known it by looking at me.

I exceeded beyond what was expected of me, which was to graduate high school as an average student, get married, have a steady job, and pop out a few kids all while keeping my husband's house clean. Instead, I graduated high school as a National Honor Society Student. I then went on to college while working full-time most days. During my senior year of college, in a down economy, I landed an internship that turned into a full-time job in Human Resources (HR) for a New York (NY) financial services firm. During that time I still worked double shifts on the weekend at the waitressing job I had had through college. I needed that job to pay for the expenses associated with the fancy New York City (NYC) job: train passes, parking passes, subway fares, suits from Ann Taylor, and the NYC *coffee, bagel, and lunch.*

I was working what many would describe as "hard"—to the point that there was no mystery where I was—either sleeping in my bed (for far too few hours); showering at home; working at the library for school, at my NY job, at my New Jersey waitressing job; or transiting to one of those locations.

I kept that pace up for about five months straight. I wasn't a workaholic. I was doing what I thought I had to do to pay my bills—to survive. When I couldn't take it anymore, I decided I was done prostituting my soul for money and corporate HR experience, so I quit the waitressing job at the end of one Sunday night shift. I didn't know what that would mean for my "real job" as I literally had no idea how I would pay for a train pass next month to get me to that "real job."

I didn't care. Enough was enough. What good was making money if I couldn't even make it to the bank to deposit the cash? Plus, the way I saw it, I wasn't going to be unemployed forever.

The Ego Is "Large and In Charge"

The very day after I quit—a Monday morning—the head of HR at the financial services firm offered me a full-time job with enough money to equal what I was making as an intern plus the money I made from waitressing. I didn't have any other plans so I said yes. I stayed at that job for six years and went from chief HR lackey to assistant vice president by twenty-five. I was making way more money than I ever imagined I would at that age. Plus I was a valued top performer. I am not exactly sure what I was valued for—probably just plain *ole* hard work. I didn't think it mattered that I didn't know what I was valued for (or so I thought). I had all the professional markers for success—the title, money, autonomy, an office, and camaraderie with my peers.

Personally I also had my own home (after having had the experience of living in Manhattan, of course), a nice new car (my second one actually), and a closet full of really nice clothes.

Basically, I got all that by saying "yes" to every opportunity that came my way:

- a new client group that would have stretched someone else beyond their capacity—"I'll take it";
- a difficult executive no one else wanted to deal with—"I'll talk to them";
- a merger with another firm—"I'll do all the mind-numbing documentation and acquisition of new employee files work";
- extra work that needed to be done ASAP—"I'll work extra hours this weekend, no problem."

I still didn't see myself as a workaholic. Instead I was doing what I thought I had to do to prove my value and worth. I wanted to be seen as a high performer so I could feel secure, valued, and successful. Yet all of that *survive, arrive, and thrive* determination had me operating at 110 percent availability to my job and at a deficit to my life, those that mattered most to me, and to my own well-being. If you had asked my family and friends, they probably would have said I had it all. Yet privately I thought I was having a nervous breakdown and I couldn't hide it anymore. I was so unhappy I couldn't control my emotions for the first time in my life. I either couldn't stop crying or I couldn't predict when the next trigger would start me crying again. I think my family and friends were stunned because for years I had a killer game face. I was happy, funny, put together, responsible, energetic, successful, and had all the answers for everyone else's problems.

I didn't even fully understand myself why this was happening.

The Flames of Burnout Emerge and Spread

I was emotionally and physically exhausted. I started losing excitement for my work, feeling the payback wasn't enough given what I was personally sacrificing. I felt unable to cope with the pace of the demands I felt were upon me at work. As well I felt defeated that I couldn't take care of the things that needed my attention in my personal life. On top of it all, I felt guilty for wanting "more" from life and for not knowing what "more" looked like. I only knew what I didn't want—the things I feared most—losing my job, losing favor with my boss and peers, losing anyone's confidence in me, and not having enough money to support myself.

Those thoughts caused me pain and even paralyzed me at times. In addition to not knowing what I wanted professionally, I didn't know what I wanted personally. All my friends were getting married and starting families. Did I want to be married? To have a family? Not having either would have been blasphemy to everyone I knew. I didn't know if I was more afraid of being alone or of becoming codependent on a husband and losing myself in motherhood.

I could relate to the joke regarding singles or lonely spouses: "Would you rather be lonely or miserable?"

I realized that *I was so busy doing* what was expected of me that I had no insight at all into who *I was*. I wasn't sure what I liked, was interested in, or what I actually wanted for my life. Because I couldn't connect with what I really wanted for my life despite all I had achieved, I was unhappy, exhausted, crabby, and felt powerless. Because I had no idea how to figure it out, I was suffering.

It was overwhelming.

I related to people who are abducted by aliens and experience "missing time." It felt like one minute I was a kid playing with my friends and Barbie Dolls, sure I would grow up to be an actress. Next, I was in an HR job in a NY financial services firm, and I wasn't quite sure how that had happened. I don't ever recall discovering who I was or what I wanted along the way. I just stumbled into it all, content that everyone else seemed pleased with "my" choices and "success."

My Choice for "A Good Life"—Whatever that Meant

Finally, I realized there was something I had accomplished all on my own. I had made all my fears a reality. I was living beyond my means, in that I had bankrupted my energy, natural optimism, and ability to get anything done that mattered to me. I didn't even know what mattered to me. Measuring with my Faith Spectrum, I was living so far over into fear (believing something bad could happen) versus hope (believing something good could happen) that I thought I could never connect to what mattered to me.

Unconsciously, I blamed it all on my job. I left it.

And three companies later, the same pattern repeated itself: come in strong, rise to top performer, feel better about myself and my life for a while, and then slowly lose interest in the job, my boss, or the people around me. Why? Because everywhere I went, I was thinking my worth was wrapped up in my ability to fulfill everyone else's dreams, expectations, and needs. It was as though having my own dreams, expectations, and needs somehow made me weak. This way of being was *not* sustainable. It was clear that I was operating over and over again on the path to burnout.

Since not making any choice had been my choice, I had to make a new choice. I chose to have a happy life, whatever that meant. Immediately, I decided to find out what *a happy life* meant to me.

CHAPTER 1

PREPARE TO PIVOT

The Focus of This Book

This book predominantly focuses on how you nurture yourself on a soul level when you are feeling overwhelmed, tired, cynical, powerless, and/or burned out. It can prepare you for awakening awareness of "your work"—the ultimate intention you have for those you serve.

If you are already feeling somewhat burned out, yet want to connect with a sense of purpose, you must first learn how to nurture and take care of yourself on a soul level. Being engaged at your job and connecting to a sense of purpose happens when you serve others. You cannot effectively serve others if you are depleted physically, emotionally, or spiritually, or your basic needs for survival are not secure. You also can't serve others in a meaningful way or effectively if you are unhappy at your job.

This book is not about changing what you think or feel about your job. It's also not about changing your job or the circumstances at your place of work. The truth is, anything your employer can do to alleviate your exhaustion, cynicism, powerlessness or burnout will *never* be more powerful than what you can learn to do for yourself. Clarity about your attitude and approach to your job might be

> Anything your employer can do to alleviate your exhaustion, cynicism, powerlessness, or burnout will never be more powerful than what you can learn to do for yourself.

a byproduct of learning how to revive your soul, heal your ego, and get them to work together more productively. No matter what dimension of engagement to burnout you are experiencing, by reading this book you are giving yourself the opportunity to reclaim that you are worthy of care and a connection to a sense of purpose. That is true no matter how contracted you have been while performing your job or how guilty you have been feeling for wanting more, despite what you have pushed yourself to tolerate or accepted as enough to be happy.

People often say, "If you can put your mind to it, you can conquer anything." This sentiment is about having an attitude that enables you to persist toward a goal. Since the main focus of this sentiment is about *conquering*, the motivation it offers suggests getting your mental state ready to experience obstacles. *Conquering* obstacles might feed your ego, but it may not feed your soul. It also might call you to sacrifice your well-being as you endure factors that can lead to burnout. I believe it's better to live by "If you put your soul in it, you can *accomplish* anything." This means put your soul in charge versus your thoughts or ego. *Accomplishing* from your soul enables

> "Are what I am offering to others, giving to myself, and habitually thinking, feeling, and doing opening a sense of accomplishment and purpose? Or a sense of burnout?"

a sustainable connection with a sense of purpose. *Conquering* for too long from your ego often steers you to the path to burnout. Making this switch can start with you asking yourself a question: "Are what I am offering to others, giving to myself, and habitually thinking, feeling, and doing opening a sense of accomplishment and purpose? Or conquering and burnout?" This book offers you the opportunity to answer these questions for yourself and shows you how self-clarity and soul-nurturing are kinder, gentler and easier ways to pivot away from the path to burnout toward the path of purpose.

How to Get the Most out of This Book

The anticipation of reading this book may have you thinking, "Oh no! I'm gonna have work to do, and I don't want to do any work because I am so overwhelmed already."

Intuitively you may sense you have to change your mindset, behavior, and feelings but you don't know how and you fear not having the energy to figure it out. If that's you, please know it's A-OK to read the book in chunks and take an approach of "try this, then try that, and see what happens." It's also okay to have a strategy of "read it, try it, learn through experiencing it, and repeat."

Just be sure to repeat. Persistence is how you achieve anything.

I promise this book offers you a method by which you will feel your ability to observe and nurture yourself returning to you. It will make you say, "I can do this!"

Here are three more things you can consider giving to yourself to help you achieve a soul-fulfilling approach to work:

1. A purpose partner
2. A list of twenty-five things
3. Journaling your journey in the *From Burnout to Purpose Workbook*

Let me explain what these are and the benefits of each.

A Purpose Partner

In reading this book, you have made me your professional coach. I will guide you on how to get connected to your sense of purpose. A purpose partner is a buddy to talk to while you read this book and try out its strategies. Securing a purpose partner can help you.

Here's why.

People are always going to put their two cents into your life for different reasons. I promise you—this will never go away. This will happen because it is what humans do to other humans they care about. The people in your pack—your peer group and especially your family—feel justified to do this. We are information-taking-in, meaning-making, sharing-our-views-with-others machines. If you don't demonstrate that you are happy and confident in the direction you are headed in, with some success to back you up, loved ones—especially family—are going to interject and try to help you. To you, it will feel like they are trying to "fix" you. Your pack may only want what is "best for you." What they cannot see is that their definition of "best for you" may not match up to yours. Yet how supported you feel by your pack often greatly influences your ability to get out of a mode where you may feel stuck or powerless to change.

There is a fable I have heard several times and I tell it to teach my clients about "the power of your pack." It's about an eagle who was raised to believe it was a chicken. I tell the story like this:

"There once was an eagle egg resting in a nest on the top of a mountain. One day an earthquake shook the mountain causing the egg to roll down to a chicken farm in the foothills below. The chickens found a hatched baby eagle and decided to raise it with their other chicks. The baby eagle soon loved his home and family, but something within him wanted to soar like the eagles he would notice in the skies above. The eagle would dream of being like the other eagles but when he shared his dream with the chickens, they thought he was silly. They assured him the best life was down on the farm versus up in the skies above.

"Eventually the eagle grew up and decided to give up his dream to live among the eagles. Instead, he lived life as the other chickens did. Eventually, the eagle died."

The moral of the story: You become what you believe you are.

As sad as it is, I love this story. I think there is so much to be learned from this eagle and his chicken family beyond the moral of the story. For one thing, it's not necessarily bad to hang out with others who have different values or ambitions than ours, but it can make it harder to feel supported in our aspirations.

Whether you are relatively happy or not in life, the people you surround yourself with matter tremendously. When they hold you in esteem, agree with your attitudes, values, choices, dreams, and ambitions, you feel good. When they don't, things start to feel icky and being around them can get really awkward really fast.

When we are undecided about who we are and what we want for our life, we become the cumulation of the people we hang out with the most. That's "the power of our pack." They will hold a lot more weight in guiding our decisions than anything else that might captivate our interest. Most of us spend too much time comparing ourselves against the norm of our peer group, which can cut us off from feeling connected with a sense of engagement, personal clarity, and purpose. When what we want or have doesn't look like what others around us want or have, it cuts off our motivation to fully discover and follow our interests and to make sense of them.

The degree to which people who are close to us are injecting their opinion into what we should be doing with our life can be a measure of how happy or stuck we seem to be. This doesn't mean we have to fly the chicken coop and leave our judgmental chickens behind. Instead, being conscious of our choice to live a life that suits us means we will need to let the people closest to us know of our choice to be someone who is fulfilled by our work and life versus drained or uninspired. That means demonstrating evidence of our determination to live connected with a sense of purpose. When we do this, we will notice support even when others don't agree with our choice. In addition, we will recognize and open up to welcoming into our life more and more people who also want to love their work and life.

Why does this matter? Because support from our peer group matters a lot—especially from those in our family. Why a family member? Because studies show that one thing you can do to get out of "occupational amotivation" is to garner support from a family member.[1] *Amotivated* describes a person who wants to do something, but may be adverse to making a choice or a commitment because they're not sure what to do and because they cannot see a link between their choices and potential outcomes. *Unmotivated* means being content with not knowing what you want to do, and being content to do nothing about it. Maybe a person doesn't have ideas about what their future could be, no confidence they can get what they want, or no knowledge about manifesting happiness and success in their life.

Close family members can help you see a relationship between making a choice and its potential positive or negative consequences. You want to expand your sense of self, recover from setbacks or trauma, or manifest new choices in life. Their support may assist in the development of your clarity, confidence, and conviction to make choices that can lead to a connection with purpose.

While you are reading this book, I want you to identify a family member (or a friend or colleague if a family member is not available) to be your purpose partner. Whether family member, friend, or colleague, this person must be someone whom you observe to be happy and fulfilled in their life and with their work. If they are retired, then consider whether they were happy with their work. If they are unemployed professionally, then perhaps you see them as happy in what they do for others in their life—whether that is volunteer work or work they do for their families. You don't have to want to be what they are or were professionally. What you want is to get aligned with the mindset of a person you aspire to understand and tap into. If there is more than one person you wish to invite into this role, that's okay too.

A purpose partner is someone whose influence you value when you are making decisions; they support you in carrying out your own choices. They are someone who is willing to listen to you without injecting judgment.

Their primary role is to *witness* your sense of clarity, confidence, and conviction for your work resurfacing. You want to surround yourself with people you believe are fulfilled and allow them to support you while you pivot toward the path of purpose.

> A personal support system from within our pack helps us to feel secure. Alienation from our pack is a very risky proposition to animals and humans alike. To secure your place in your pack, you must communicate with others what you are up to or they will continue to relate to you as the overwhelmed, tired, cynical, power-drained, or burned-out person you were.

A personal support system from within our pack helps us to feel secure. Alienation from our pack is a very risky proposition to animals and humans alike. To secure your place in your pack, you must communicate with others what you are up to or they will continue to relate to you as the overwhelmed, tired, cynical, power-drained, or burned-out person you were.

I suggest you schedule a set time of about fifteen minutes for your purpose partner to listen to you. It might make sense to meet with them when you complete a chapter. Find a structure for meeting that makes sense and feels right for you. As you read this book and practice what you are learning, adding in a meeting with your purpose partner will be like going to the gym more often. You know you will develop your muscles and strength faster when you do that. It's the same with learning and practicing the principles in this book.

I suggest you connect with your purpose partner via phone, FaceTime, or in person to share these five ideas with them:

1. What stuck with you most from the chapter. Teach them the concept. No need to read from the book or your notes; just teach what you remember. What you remember is what you need to absorb most.

2. What you're most excited to put into practice from the chapter. What do you find encouraging about what you learned or

observed about yourself? Share a story about something you practiced and experienced a challenge or success with.

3. What you're challenged by or confused about from the chapter. What are you reluctant to try? What are you frustrated with, because it's not working the way you thought it would work? Maybe share what hurts to hear. This might be something you are feeling guilty about or something you don't want to try or deal with. Share a story about something you practiced but were challenged by.

4. What you observed about yourself when reading this chapter and practicing its concepts. What did you observe about yourself when you read something from this book or when you put something you learned into practice?

5. A request for additional support or help you would welcome from your purpose partner.

The purpose partner's only role is to listen and bear witness to your transformation. They don't have to be counselors, therapists, or even a person who reads this book. Again, they are there to listen to you and be a witness to your healing and growth. If they want to share their thoughts about the book's content or share a personal experience from their own life, that is fine. But they don't have to share. Your purpose partner doesn't need to offer any words of wisdom or to agree.

There are several benefits to having a purpose partner alongside you while you read and practice the concepts that this book teaches:

- **Accountability**—You will give yourself the best support to ensure your success is possible. It helps to have someone in your life you will report to about your progress. Built-in accountability can help you stay on course with your healing and growth.

- **Support for your success**—A witness to your transformation will give you someone who supports your new outlook. When you are done reading this book, you will be on a path to connecting with a sense of purpose. If no one around you knows about the work you are doing in this area of your life, you will still have people around you who relate to you as the person who is burned out, hates your job, or just feels stuck. That won't help you to feel like the genuine eagle you are and aspire to be seen as while you make a meaningful contribution in the world. People are much more vested when they feel as though they are a part of a change versus when they are told about a change.

- **A new conversation in your life**—Give yourself at least one person in your life for whom the conversation shifts from complaining and venting about what you hate about your job or life situation to talking about what you want to create. Plus, in having a purpose partner, we are more likely to retain what we share with or teach to another. There was probably a time in your life when you knew the Pythagorean theorem. You knew it because you were taught it and were surrounded by others who were also talking about it. When the discussion went away, you forgot all about it.

  Keep the conversation about what you want to create alive by having another to share in it with you. Time spent talking about what you want to create takes from time you would have spent talking about what you don't want. Whatever we are talking about is what is real for us and alive in our life, and it is what we have the capacity to see evidence of its happening.

- **Feedback**—When you share with your purpose partner what you are getting from what you are learning and applying from this book, you can ask for and receive supportive feedback from someone who knows, likes, and even loves you on a personal level.

- **Help others as you help yourself**—Sharing what you are learning and experiencing offers your purpose partner an opportunity to have some breakthroughs of their own. Most people who are happy with their work probably got there unwittingly. When you meet with your purpose partner, you will find that they will relate to much of what you share and may even recall times when they made choices relative to what you are learning about. They probably didn't realize at the time that their choice mattered as much as it did. Give your purpose partner insight into what they perhaps did unwittingly that served them well.

If you don't know what to say to enroll someone as your purpose partner, here are some suggested talking points:

- I recently started reading a book called *From Burnout to Purpose* to help me learn how to heal from (or avoid) job burnout so that I can find a connection to a sense of purpose through my work. I am doing this because I want to _____ (share why the book appeals to you).

- The author of the book *From Burnout to Purpose* suggests that I ask someone to be my purpose partner—someone who I believe enjoys happiness and success in their life including what they do for a living. Sharing with a purpose partner can help me get on a path to feeling a deeper connection with my work.

- I would like you to be this person because I observe you to be someone who is happy with your life, seems to love what you do for a living, and would be a good listener and a witness to my journey. I see you as having a mindset and outlook that I aspire to understand and have. Primarily, I'd like someone in my life who can witness the change I want to make and who can relate to me as someone who is up to something more meaningful. I no longer want to be a person who isn't happy with their work or work environment. I want to create happiness and success in my life and my work.

- If you agree to help me it will involve connecting live with me for about fifteen minutes after I read through each chapter. I will explain what I am learning and the experiences and observations I am having while practicing what I am learning.

- You don't have to share your own experiences if you don't want to. And you definitely don't have to read the book or "fix" me. You can best help me by giving me your attention and support while I make my own choices. Even if you don't agree with those choices I believe you are someone who can support me in achieving a more fulfilling outlook for my work and in my life.

- Is that a role you would be willing to play?

If they agree to be your purpose partner—great! Thank them and set up one or two standing appointments to speak about what you are learning and experiencing while you practice the concepts you learn from this book.

If they don't agree to be your purpose partner, thank them for considering it and ask if they have a suggestion for who you might work with. Move on to the next person and keep going until you find a purpose partner you are comfortable with.

If you don't know of anyone who can be your purpose partner, stay on the lookout for one, but don't let not securing a purpose partner stop you from moving forward with reading the book and practicing its concepts. It will never be too late to share your story of pivoting from a path to burnout to a path of purpose when the perfect purpose partner shows up in your life.

A List of Twenty-Five Things

I counsel my private clients to create a list of twenty-five things that they enjoy doing or experiencing. Finding more than twenty-five things becomes too overwhelming and the list will be diluted with

> What nurtures the soul also tends to nurture the ego—it doesn't work the other way around. When you are feeding your soul, the things you do offer you a sense of peace, fulfillment, happiness, confidence, energy, and growth.

activities that don't really matter. Finding fewer than twenty-five things becomes an exercise a client can dismiss. Some people don't reach twenty-five, but it's a challenge to strive for. I recommend you try this.

The real challenge here is to create the list while directly observing yourself in the act of nurturing your soul—not just your ego.

What nurtures the soul also tends to nurture the ego—it doesn't work the other way around. When you are feeding your soul, the things you do offer you a sense of

1. **peace**: you feel relaxed, restful, comfortable, hopeful, patient, accepting of imperfections, civil even in the face of confrontation or adversity, cooperative with others, and attentive to how others cooperate with you;

2. **fulfillment**: you feel satisfied, positive, thrilled, prosperous, thankful, and enjoy a sense of work-life balance;

3. **happiness**: you notice you are smiling, laughing, being humorous, having fun, being enthusiastic, engaging, and interacting socially or playfully with others versus doing any of these things at the expense of others;

4. **confidence**: you observe that you are centered, empowered, aware of what you have to offer that can make a difference, feeling open or safe to go outside your comfort zone, being interactive and social yet able to set and respect boundaries in relationships, taking care of yourself, and easily offering praise or gratitude to others;

5. **energy**: you feel motivated, have physical and mental energy, and accomplish things you want to get done; you are thinking *big*, and seeing possibilities;

6. **growth**: you are interested in learning, improving, and rec-ognizing the good despite the negative in yourself, others, or situations.

Get started on observing yourself for these six feeling experiences now. Add to your list as you have these experiences during the natural course of life versus writing the list from memory. Part of this exer-cise is to strengthen your ability to observe yourself. Your experiences don't have to be related to work. In fact, the simpler the experience, the better. Maybe you were watching a funny movie, chatting with a cher-ished friend, enjoying your favorite tea, playing a game with a child, snuggling with your beloved pet, praying, meditating, working out, spending time in nature, or working for your favorite charity.

Be sure to include things on your list you know you can do or experience without undue expenditure of funds, time, or dependency on others. Skydiving might be very thrilling for you, but after a tough day at work when you usually don't even have the energy to flip a few cutlets and make a salad before donning your favorite sweatpants and turning on Netflix, I doubt you will have the time or energy to find an airplane you can jump out of.

You can create this list of twenty-five things right in your smart phone in a notes app. If not, *good ole* paper and pen will do. Just keep the list with you.

If you can do something for yourself every day to get started on developing your list you will be on the path toward your recovery by practicing soul care. Not doing so can continue to block your ability to keep a sense of clarity, confidence, and conviction for your work and life.

The Workbook

As you read this book, I will ask you questions. I will invite you to consider the magnitude to which you relate to one concept or another.

I will ask you to meet with a *purpose partner* and complete the *list of twenty-five things*. Should you choose to engage in such activities and give yourself the best opportunity possible to get the most out of the time and money you invested to read this book, you might want to make it as easy as possible to do so.

Here are a few of the advantages of having the *From Burnout to Purpose Workbook* handy while you read this book and practice its concepts:

- You will have a chapter-by-chapter recap of the key concepts I share. You have no time to re-read the book? No problem! Just use your workbook to refresh your memory of the key concepts. Go back to the book if you would like to refresh yourself with the full details.

- You will have one place to remember your journey from burn-out to purpose. It's like a diary or journal that you can look back on to remember your triggers, strategies for care, and successes.

- You will have an opportunity to write down your thoughts and remember the concepts that impressed you most. When we write we tend to come from the heart. When we type, we tend to come from the head. When you are healing and evolving and want more meaningful results, it's best to invite the heart into the process.

- You will have a place to record your sessions with your purpose partner. I offer you questions to ask them and having a workbook gives you a place to jot your notes down from those discussions.

Having the *Workbook* just makes doing the work easier and shifting from the path to burnout to the path of purpose more expedient. In short, it just makes everything easier, faster, and more enjoyable for you!

You can get the workbook I created to help you capture your journey from the path to burnout to the path of purpose at www.fromburnouttopurpose.com.

In a Job You Hate? Yay! It's the Perfect Time to Pivot

I know that right now—being in your current job situation—you may be feeling completely drained, much less be feeling a sense of purpose. However, being in a less-than-ideal job may be the perfect place for you to start on your journey toward a sense of purpose. Let me explain why.

When you begin to practice soul care in situations that feel draining, your action becomes a "grand gesture." Grand gestures accelerate your ability to notice and act on opportunities to feel connected to a sense of purpose.

I love to use an analogy to explain this concept so you can absorb it deeply. If you have ever seen the movie *Pretty Woman* with Richard Gere and Julia Roberts, you will get this concept in a snap! Richard plays a conservative, emotionally guarded, business professional who has certain phobias (mostly fueled by doing anything outside his comfort zone). Imagine you are him. Julia plays a fearless, free-spirited prostitute who settles for nothing less than what she wants. Imagine she is your connection to a sense of purpose.

> Grand gestures accelerate your ability to notice and act on opportunities to feel connected to a sense of purpose.

Under very unconventional and dysfunctional circumstances (the job that's draining you), they find each other, fall in love, and the question becomes what to do about it. Neither of them is very good at walking away from something they want. He wants her and she wants a fairy-tale romance that demonstrates his commitment to her (even though she gets it that a commitment is probably way out of his comfort zone so the fairy-tale thing will be highly unlikely to happen).

In the end, he goes to her unglamorous apartment (the place of employment you hate) to win her back. He arrives in a white limo (his version of a white horse), climbs up her fire escape (even though he is afraid of heights), professes his feelings (any talk of feelings is way outside his comfort zone), and wins her love (the connection to a sense of purpose).

If he did things within his comfort zone (i.e., called her on the phone, sent someone to her apartment with flowers and asked her to meet him back in Beverly Hills—his comfort zone), he wouldn't have won her over. He got her attention immediately because of their con-flicted situation and because he demonstrated that he was ready to offer her what she needed to feel cherished—not just what would make him comfortable, given his circumstances. Plus, he was authentic with his offer. He was happy climbing out of the roof of the limo with flowers and smiling as he climbed up that fire escape. He wasn't sweating, whining, and saying, "I hate being out of my comfort zone," "I hate climbing up a fire escape ladder," "This is hard and scary." He was giving off energy that resonated with being in love (connected to a sense of purpose), despite the external factors. What was unspoken and only shown by his actions, despite the circumstances and the setting, was how serious and ready he was to have her in his life. And she was rooting him on the whole way up that fire escape ladder and "rescuing him right back." So the return he got for offering her what she needed was that he aligned himself with the very same reward—he too received what made him feel cherished, valuable, and worthy of stepping out of his comfort zone.

> Offering what you have to offer without regard for the less-than-ideal circumstances you are in is how you make a "grand gesture."

Offering what you have to offer without regard for the less-than-ideal circumstances you are in is how you make a "grand gesture." Such a move gives you power, velocity, and visibility with the energy of the universe. Nurturing yourself through a less-than-ideal circumstance is a fast route to a sense of purpose. It's faster than when you are in a circumstance you feel lukewarm about. Compare being "in like" with being "in love." Being "in like" can be comfortable as it's not too risky. When we are comfortable we are often not inspired to make "grand gesture" moves to find a situation we can "love."

If you are in a job situation that's diminishing your soul, you have a grand-gesture opportunity to no longer be part of the less-than-engaged workforce. The truth is, less than one-third of the US workforce has never been reported to be engaged since Gallup began tracking the employee engagement levels of the US working population in 2000.[2] That number is even lower outside the US. In 2020 Gallup reported that the US engagement rate fluctuated between 31 through 40 percent.[3] The recent fluctuations are no doubt worker reactions to economic and world events such as racial injustices, the COVID-19 pandemic, and political divide—more so than changes in organizational strategies and programs. Regardless of the reasons for the fluctuations, are we really happy as a nation with a workforce where at best only 40 percent of us are engaged?

At this point, you are probably asking yourself a few questions around the concepts of engagement and burnout:

- "What does it mean to be *engaged* at work?"
- "Is it possible for me to be *engaged* and get on *the path of purpose* given my current situation?"
- "What is *burnout*?"
- "Am I already on *the path to burnout*?"
- "Am I really *burned out*?"

Let's look at burnout, engagement, and the states or dimensions in between.

CHAPTER 2

AM I BURNED OUT AND DON'T KNOW IT?

What Is Burnout? Tell It to Me Straight

Christina Maslach, PhD, an American social psychologist and professor emerita of psychology at the University of California, Berkeley, is co-creator of Maslach Burnout Inventory™ and Areas of Worklife Survey assessment tools, as well as several books and articles on burnout.[4] She is well-known for her research on burnout, job stress, individuation, and social influence. Michael P. Leiter, PhD, is an organizational psychologist, consultant on preventing burnout and building work engagement, adjunct professor at Saint Mary's University, and a former professor of Industrial and Organizational Psychology at Deakin University. He also served for over thirty years as the Canada Research Chair in Occupational Health and Wellbeing at Acadia University. Maslach and Leiter have partnered on several publications on burnout. Together they define *burnout* as "a psychological syndrome emerging as a prolonged response to chronic interpersonal stressors on the job." Other experts characterize burnout as a negative attitude, which may include apathy toward your job or toward the people you interact with at your job.

In May 2019, the World Health Organization (WHO) classified *burnout* as an occupational phenomenon. That means, even though it is not a medical condition, people who experience burnout may seek medical guidance. WHO reports,

> *Burn-out is a syndrome conceptualized as resulting from chronic workplace stress that has not been successfully managed. It is characterized by three dimensions:*

> - *feelings of energy depletion or exhaustion;*
> - *increased mental distance from one's job, or feelings of negativism or cynicism related to one's job; and*
> - *reduced professional efficacy.*[5]

Dr. Maslach and Dr. Leiter identified three situations connected with burnout. They are "Overextended (high on exhaustion only), Disengaged (high on cynicism only), and Ineffective (high on inefficacy only)."[6]

Engagement, burnout, and the three dimensions of burnout can be described as:

- **engaged**—regularly experiencing vigor, civility, and a sense of personal power to make a meaningful contribution to others. Engagement is experienced because there is clarity of who you are (on the ego and soul levels) and what you wish to enable for others as well as for yourself. There is an alignment between your values and the values of your profession and workplace.

- **overextended**—chronic overwhelm with mental and physical exhaustion predominately due to changes in the workload. This can express itself as a chronic feeling of tiredness or diminished resilience, excitement, or interest for your job.

- **disengaged**—chronic overwhelm with a cynical attitude about your job, or the people you interact with at your job.

This can be expressed as a negative or abrasive attitude, isolating or withdrawing from others, or acting with apathy toward your job.

- **ineffective**—chronic overwhelm with a feeling of powerlessness to take care of things that have meaning to you at your job. This can be expressed as low morale; struggling to accept, adjust, or cope with circumstances at your job; and perhaps suffering if you can't see how to end or change the situation.

- **burnout**—chronic mental and physical exhaustion, cynicism, and powerlessness. There is a disconnect between what has meaning for you and how to make a meaningful contribution to others.

Burnout and its intermediate dimensions are symptoms of harboring an inadequate counterbalance of what fills us up on a soul level and diminishing or silencing, consciously or not, the hunger to satisfy our soul for too long. We know we have allowed it too long because we feel stuck and powerless to change the situation. Feeling stuck is a big red flag that we have unconsciously been working with the ego in charge for too long. A lack of balance over time enables confusion, not only about what we want, but eventually over who we are. A lack of self-clarity depletes confidence in ourself and our choices, which robs our fulfillment from taking action on anything we want to achieve or even what we may routinely do in the name of self-care.

In addition to diminished energy, patience with others, and/or confidence at work, have you stopped spending time with the people who matter to you, preparing healthy meals, working out, keeping your space neat and organized, paying attention to how you look, or keeping yourself groomed? That could be an indication that you are less than engaged in your life as well as at your job. In essence, burnout

> Burnout is born from too little hope, enthusiasm, and personal clarity.

is born from too little hope, enthusiasm, and personal clarity. Burnout justifies giving priority to what might be a threat to you in some way. It steals your ability to validate your soul and nurture yourself when you are feeling depleted. Nurturing yourself when you are depleted enables you to more vividly experience creating meaning for yourself and others versus veering off onto a path to burnout.

Recent reports identify that 10% to 15% of employees are actually burned out.[7] The state of flux we are in right now—with engagement vacillating between 30% to 40%—leaves more than half the workforce falling within one or more of the intermediate dimensions. We must educate, observe, and nurture ourselves about this phenomenon, so that as a collective workforce we pivot away from burnout and return to working with purpose.

What Triggers a Fall from Engagement?

For some, pivoting away from engagement and purpose may feel like a subtle process of "falling out of love" with your job. Maybe you've stayed too long at that job and the best you can do is go through the daily and weekly motions. Perhaps you develop a "wait-and-see attitude" toward aspects of your job—meaning you might hold back from investing too much time, effort, or energy because you prefer to see how things play out. Over time, your outlook on life is likely to match your bland or cautious outlook about your job or work environment.

A shift from engagement in our work environment may be triggered by *perceived or actual* threatening situations. We believe that certain situations, rather than how we care for ourselves and respond to these situations, are more powerful for keeping us engaged. My friend Dana Lee, a diet recovery and mindset coach, says it so well: "It's not dark times that challenge you—it's your own self-limiting beliefs to face those dark times that challenge you." In other words, you don't trust yourself to be aware and nurturing of yourself, no matter what happens. You also don't trust yourself to not feel judged or guilty if you were to nurture yourself.

Specific threatening situations at work can leave us vulnerable for drifting toward burnout,[8] including these:

- undesirable or enhanced workload demands plus a lack of resources,
- loss of control over or influence on work peers,
- lack of fulfillment or rewards from the job including diminished returns on personally invested resources,
- unsupportive relationships at work,
- unfair treatment at work,
- conflicting values such as between you and your peers, the workplace culture, organizational policies, or the nature of your job or industry.

Over my years working as an HR executive, I have spoken with many employees who experienced a slight downward shift in their attitude or job performance. They would often use a variation of the word "overwhelmed" to describe their situation. For example, a change in resources or workload is *becoming unmanageable* for them; a new boss and their different approach is *suppressive* or *overpowering*; or the outcome of a situation is *hard to swallow* or *tough to take* or *unfair*. I have heard people say they are feeling "overwhelmed" in so many different ways it would be *overwhelming* to list them all here. I believe *overwhelmed* is a state between engagement and the dimensions of burnout. I define being overwhelmed as follows: to think, feel, or behave in a way to protect or serve primarily yourself. Overwhelm is experienced perhaps because you're unsure about how to make a meaningful contribution to others; because you only have clarity for what you *don't* want to happen for yourself or others (versus what you *do* want to happen); or because you become distracted by demanding circumstances.

It's losing sight of your ability to serve others while knowing and honoring your values.

Traditionally, we relate to *overwhelm* when we feel like we are just *very busy*. It might be believed to be a state that we can easily tolerate because it will last for a short period of time. We believe there's nothing we need to do to replenish ourselves while we work a few late nights to catch up on work, complete an ad hoc project, get through a busy season, and so on. However, I believe there is a shadow side to overwhelm. Under the surface of that busy business, we might become seduced by the anticipated feeling of relief that comes from *catching up* or *accomplishing* something. Chasing the anticipated high from conquering overwhelm might distract us from making a difference for others. When we do nothing to acknowledge and nurture ourselves through periods of overwhelm, we unwittingly veer away from being engaged with our work.

> Chasing the anticipated high from conquering overwhelm might distract us from making a difference for others.

You might be thinking you're not overwhelmed just because you don't make the service and protection of others a priority over protecting or serving yourself. However, to be human is to make a meaningful difference for others. It is the essence of how we evolve, self-actualize, and experience purpose with sustainable fulfillment.

Those who don't feel connected to a sense of purpose usually struggle to have regard for others. They may be thwarted in their capacity to do so because of serious circumstances affecting their life or health. In such circumstances it no doubt makes sense to make securing your basic needs and restoring yourself the priority. It might also be due to early influences or conditioning that formed the personality. In such circumstances the ego (regard for the self) is *large and in charge*. When the ego is in charge, the soul (regard for others) has been diminished or silenced. As a result, we stunt our ability to engage or to connect to a sense of purpose and lasting fulfillment. As soon as we acknowledge the overwhelm and choose to address it,

> Engagement, which bridges our connection to purpose and sustainable fulfillment, happens when making a difference for others is the primary concern.

we restore our capacity for engagement. Engagement, which bridges our connection to purpose and sustainable fulfillment, happens when making a difference for others is the primary concern.

Ignoring prolonged overwhelm can be a perfect breeding ground for overextension, disengagement, ineffectiveness, and/or burnout to emerge. These are evidenced by their primary symptoms—exhaustion, cynicism, powerlessness, or all three respectively. Ignoring overwhelm is like letting the flame under a pot on the kitchen stove burn too high for too long. Doing so can invite a dimension of burnout to emerge. Once one dimension of burnout emerges, we begin to smell something burning in the kitchen. That smell can signal there are problems developing related to how connected you may feel to your job. Once one dimension of burnout happens, we are more vulnerable to multiple dimensions emerging. For example, exhaustion *plus* cynicism. Ignore two dimensions of burnout for too long and eventually you will see and smell smoke.

Burnout is born once we are experiencing all three states at the same time—overextension, disengagement, *and* ineffectiveness. Once all three are experienced, the kitchen is on fire and it must be attended to before it spreads throughout the house. Ignoring burnout would be like ignoring the smell of something burning, the presence of smoke, and the actual flames in the kitchen. Prolonged burnout can lead to physical and emotional health problems—similar to the kitchen fire spreading throughout your home. When you experience all three signs of a fire you wouldn't remain skeptical and see if the problem resolves itself. You'd get yourself and your loved ones out of that situation immediately!

It's the same with burnout.

In short, once we experience a symptom and we believe that power to heal from it is outside ourselves, over time, we evolve into the corresponding dimension of burnout. It looks like this:

primary symptom (exhaustion) + a belief that solutions are outside our ability or control + time = the dimension of burnout (overextension)

Or

primary symptom (cynicism) + a belief that solutions are outside our ability or control + time = the dimension of burnout (disengagement)

Or

primary symptom (powerlessness) + a belief that solutions are outside our ability or control + time = the dimension of burnout (ineffectiveness)

When we enable one of those dimensions and do nothing to heal ourselves from it, we become susceptible to multiple dimensions of burnout. It looks like this:

overextension + a primary symptom (cynicism) + a belief that solutions are outside our ability or control + time = two dimensions of burnout (overextension + disengagement)

Or

overextension + a primary symptom (powerlessness) + a belief that solutions are outside our ability or control + time = two dimensions of burnout (overextension + ineffectiveness)

Or

disengagement + a primary symptom (powerlessness) + a belief that solutions are outside our ability or control + time = two dimensions of burnout (disengagement + ineffectiveness)

When we enable two dimensions and do nothing to heal ourselves from them, we become susceptible to burnout. That's when the third symptom sets in and becomes chronic as well. It looks like this:

dimensions (disengagement + ineffectiveness) + symptom (tiredness) + a belief that solutions are outside our ability or control + time = burnout

Or

dimensions (overextension+ ineffectiveness) + symptom (cynicism) + a belief that solutions are outside our ability or control + time = burnout

Or

dimensions (overextension + disengagement) + symptom (powerlessness) + a belief that solutions are outside our ability or control + time = burnout

Remember, what happens at work isn't the primary thing that makes us vulnerable to overwhelm and the dimensions of burnout. It's a lack of trusting ourself to be aware and nurturing ourself when we are experiencing overwhelm and the dimensions of burnout that matter most. After all, we can't always control what happens in our external work environment. The first step to taking care of ourselves is to observe and acknowledge changes in our level of engagement at work.

Feeling Exhausted, Cynical or Powerless at Your Job?

There is a primary symptom for each dimension of burnout—mental and physical exhaustion alone relative to your job is a state of overextension; cynicism alone is a state of disengagement; and powerlessness alone is a state of ineffectiveness. Let's look at each of the three symptoms individually.

Mental and Physical Exhaustion

*Everything seems to be exhausting me. No matter how much
I sleep or how much coffee I drink or how long I lie down,
something inside me seems to have given up. My soul is tired.*

Unknown

Every working person has probably experienced exhaustion at some
point in their career. Feeling tired of your job? Do you experience
depleted mental or physical energy due to helplessness, futility, or
tiredness due to overwork? Do you fear that you may be tired beyond
recovery? Did you ever think that maybe it's your soul that's tired?

We all feel tired from time to time. Sometimes, we just need more
sleep. Sometimes, we are coming down with a cold or dealing with a
bigger health issue. Sometimes, we have been working too hard or our
workload has gotten out of control.

If chronic exhaustion is evident for
you, the first thing to do is see your doctor. Once anything physical is ruled out, it
might be time to consider whether your
soul is tired. Could that be the reason you
experience a general malaise of "tired-

> If chronic exhaustion is
> evident for you, the first
> thing to do is see your
> doctor.

ness" that seems to follow you one day after another, no matter how
much sleep you get?

This kind of tiredness might be a mixture of a few key ingredients:

- **A cup of too much to do:** Is your workload out of control?

- **A handful of low energy:** Maybe you're just not feelin' that *pep
  in your step* and you're too mentally exhausted to figure out why.

- **A tablespoon of futility:** Does every aspect of life seem to constantly be tugging at you? Especially your job, your house, your
  family and friends, and your health? Does it feel like all of them

want more from you than you have to give, and often, are many of them tugging at you at the same time?

- **A teaspoon of bruised ego:** What detrimental meaning about yourself do you infer from the situation you're in, from what others do or say, from how you compare yourself to some past or younger version of yourself, or from how you compare yourself to any of your peers and what they have accomplished?

- **A dash of boredom**(optional): Does every day look the same? Do you crave for something "exciting" to happen yet wonder what excitement would even look like?

Mixed altogether—you might feel downright exhausted—your spark, fire and even resilience are just gone.

When I worked in corporate HR earlier in my career, I would often wish I could just sleep all day. The truth was I felt this way pretty much every day and I doubted that anything could help me to rally, get productive, or feel energetic. For my ego (which wanted to be seen as strong and right), it was enough that I could push myself to go through the motions of what I "had to do" each day. What else could I do but endure this self-inflicted abuse and place the blame outside of myself (my job, my boss, my commute, somehow my innocent mother). Can you relate?

- Do you feel tired before you go to work (even if you slept well the night before)?

- Do you anticipate that you will be drained physically and emotionally by events that will surely come up at work each day?

- Do you doubt you will have the energy to deal effectively with your workload each day (no less accomplish a few goals)?

- Even if you had the energy, do you doubt that your energy and efforts would make a difference?

- Do you feel emotionally drained after your work day?

- Do you believe others are expecting you to push yourself hard, just the way you do each day?

If you answered YES to most of these questions, you may have (or be on the brink of) work exhaustion. This type of exhaustion is characterized by feeling tired, weak, depleted of energy, lethargic, overworked, and/or overwhelmed by your workload. In addition, you notice you can't bounce back like maybe you could in the past.

Exhaustion can start as subtly as not wanting to get out of bed to go to work. Now we all experience that feeling from time to time but when it happens more often than not, it can be an indicator that you might be on your way to joining the burnout club. In addition to not wanting to get out of bed, prolonged focus on or exposure to any of the following examples *without taking remedial action* may leave you at greater risk for work exhaustion:

- **Abusive leadership**—we all know what it feels like to work for a jerk of a boss. Here are some specifics: verbal abuse, breaking promises, placing blame, displaced anger, rudeness, and sharing negative emotions. Charming, isn't it? Do you tolerate it?

- **Low physical activity**—even though just fifteen minutes of fitness a day can work wonders, do you insist you just don't have the time for a regular routine?

- **Obesity**—do you understand it's time to seriously consider foods that actually nurture your body versus those that just fill your belly and soothe your ego, and yet you just don't have it in you to make different choices?

- **Diminished resources**—do you chronically feel expected to perform amazing feats of accomplishment without adequate resources? Is your workload simply expecting you to do too much with too little?

- **Withdrawal tendencies**—do you use avoidance as a method for dealing with unresolved issues? For example, do you avoid socializing with your friends and peers? Note: complaining about your job doesn't count as socializing. I know it feels like it's bonding with others, especially those who are also unhappy, but it doesn't give you any points toward achieving a sense of purpose.

- **Low job involvement**—are you doing the absolute least amount you have to do to get the job done?

- **A desire to quit**—do you ever feed a fantasy about pulling a Jerry McGuire or having a hero show up on a white horse to rescue you from your job?

So you can see from this partial list that it's not all your boss's, co-worker's, client's, or work culture's fault. Sure what they spew in your direction matters and their support can help fill the cracks in your soul. However, they are not fully the remedy that can *heal* your less-than-engaged state. How you respond to others and how you heal what's wounded in your soul are directly in your control AND THIS IS GOOD NEWS! Anything that is actually in our control is always good news. The second you accept that it's possible for you to control whether or not you will heal your job-related exhaustion, you pivot toward purpose and away from burnout.

Cynicism

> *For true happiness, it's best to look within yourself rather than rely on others or the world around you. The sad but true fact is that it's difficult to be happy if you rely on outside sources. The root of happiness is joy, and joy lives within you. It's not influenced by external events.*

Keith Harrell

Has your regard gone down for the things you are responsible for? Do you frequently have a negative or cynical attitude toward others or about things you have to do? Do you seek to face your cynicism? Or do you remove yourself from situations or people that ignite your cynicism whenever you can?

Cynicism is a state of mind that believes others are only motivated by self-interest. It's being in a regular state of skepticism, pessimism, or doubt that things will work out well or be as valuable as they promise to be. Merriam-Webster defines a cynic as "a person who has negative opinions about other people and about the things people do."

The strongest indicator that we might be headed for burnout (or are already there and just in denial of our symptoms) is cynicism. This is further influenced by how exhausted we are. Cynicism at its core is grounded in an egocentric focus. Our ego pulls us away from connecting to a sense of fulfillment from anyone or anything, including our job. Cynicism directs undue negative focus to how we feel about others, making us believe more in what's not possible (or the bad that could happen). It affects our ability to make a meaningful connection socially or professionally with peers and customers. It is projected by a low self-worth, a reduced sense of work fulfillment, and/or poor job performance.

> The strongest indicator that we might be headed for burnout is cynicism, which at its core is grounded in an ego-centric focus.

How dedicated would you say you are to your job? How dedicated would you say you are to your customers, your co-workers, your supervisors, the people you interact with? We all have customers, but sadly we often regard our only customer as our boss or the person buying the product or service of the company we work for. We cannot overlook any of the people we interact with as being customers of what our soul has to offer and still feel connected to a sense of purpose. You must see everyone you interact with as a customer—from the person who delivers your lunch to the CEO. Do you believe each person could be better off from having interacted with you?

When it comes to job satisfaction, did you know that how you feel about the people you interact with has more to do with how satisfied you feel about your job than if you are interested in the tasks you perform in that job?[9]

As we all know, we are not meant to please everyone all the time. And everyone is not meant to please us all the time, although we often live life with a belief that how others treat us is justification for how we treat them. With that, we experience cynicism from time to time. Someone will do or say something that makes us contort our face into the same shape it would make if we smelled something really foul and a cartoon bubble might appear over our head that reads "WTF?" Emotionally, we might respond with some form of fear—anger, hurt, shame, confusion, judgment.

Evolved consciousness calls our norm to accept others, forgive ourselves, and feel gratitude for moving forward with refined boundaries and a deeper, stronger sense of relatedness and connection with others. But sometimes our cynicism builds up and we respond to others or situations we encounter with a degree of reserve, expecting the same reaction, outcome, or pain we might have experienced in the past. The quote by Keith Harrell that opens this passage means that positive attitudes come from within. Negative attitudes come from being focused on what's happening around you and what you fear might happen, perhaps because something similar happened in the past. Being overwhelmed by such focus and consistency in that way of thinking eventually leads us to develop a cynical attitude as our norm or to just withdraw altogether. This is how cynicism evolves.

If you're feeling cynical about your job or work environment, don't focus on things changing in your job to restore your mood. Focus on observing yourself and on strengthening your relationships.

Our degree of cynicism is directly related to the degree to which we are willing to observe and nurture ourselves plus to have an emotional involvement with those we interact with. This results in the degree to which you will offer and accept support and care from others and from yourself. When cynicism becomes a relatively normal state, you are most vulnerable to burnout.

Is being cynical your norm? Consider the following questions:

- Are there people or situations you consistently offer a negative, cold, indifferent, or impersonal attitude toward?

- Are there people or situations you tend to emotionally withdraw from and/or actively avoid when possible?

- Are you interested in finding fault or do you place blame on others? How often do you hear yourself asking, "Who did this?" or "Who is responsible for this?" as a knee-jerk reaction to a newly discovered problem?

- Do you doubt your contributions really make a difference for others?

- Do you perceive others as having a destructive style (berating, bullying, abrasive, obtrusive, unsupportive, or avoiding responsibility)?

- Do you frequently talk about what some "idiot" did to those who are not directly involved in or capable of solving said idiocy?

If you answered YES to most of these questions, you may be practicing *cynicism*. As with exhaustion, how you respond to others and how you heal what's wounded in your soul is directly in your control. Again, the second you accept that it's possible for you to control whether or not you will heal your cynicism, you pivot away from burnout and toward purpose.

Powerlessness

> *You have the power to heal your life, and you need to know that. We think so often that we are helpless, but we're not. We always have the power of our minds ... Claim and consciously use your power.*

Louise Hay

Do you feel incompetent, insufficient, discouraged, or powerless to do what you want to do or accomplish?

How much would you agree with these statements?

- I accomplish things that really matter to me every day at my job.
- I have the resources I need to get my work done.
- I feel supported and encouraged at my job by my colleagues.
- I value my work contributions.
- Others value my work contributions.
- I feel qualified to do my job.
- I feel I can handle anything that may come up in my job.
- It's okay to contribute to others in my unique way.
- My contributions make a meaningful difference for others.
- I address issues that come up related to my work or workplace.

If you have a low degree of agreement with many of these statements, you may be feeling powerless at your job. This can lead to being ineffective, developing additional states of burnout, and eventually burnout.

> Feeling powerless at work can directly affect the quality of your work.

Feeling powerless at work is especially common. It is concerning, however, because it can directly affect the quality of your work. We all know that when the quality of our work falls, we stand out and not in a good way. In my experience, management tends to tolerate a degree of exhaustion (most of us empathize with feeling that way from time to time). Management also tolerates some cynicism from workers who are still producing strong results—at least until someone with a more energetic, positive outlook who can also produce results shows up. But when you don't produce, then your boss isn't producing. That's a problem that quickly gets noticed.

Although there are things organizations do to improve an employee's ability to recover from feeling powerless, often it's left to the individual to "shape up or ship out." Often, when an organization claims it is "doing its part," it means it is carrying out performance counseling. This might include giving the employee "a talking to," a poor job performance review, written documentation, and/or a demotion. Threats of those things come your way to put you on notice that you need to improve.

So, do you feel as though everyone else's agenda runs your day and you can't get anything done at work? Welcome to powerlessness. As with exhaustion and cynicism, how you respond to others and how you heal what's wounded in your soul are directly in your control. Again, the second you accept that it's possible for you to control whether or not you will heal your sense of powerlessness, you pivot away from burnout toward purpose.

Burnout Recovery Matters for Your Life—Literally!

Exhaustion, cynicism, and powerlessness are the primary symptoms that signal you are in one or more dimension of burnout. Prolonged burnout often brings on physical issues that can lead to serious health threats if they are not tended to medically. If you think you are heading toward, or are already in, job burnout, the first and most important thing to do is consult with a medical professional, especially if you are already experiencing physical symptoms. Most people will easily admit to feeling "stressed." I believe "stress" is corporate jargon for "fear." Trying to achieve engagement, success, or fulfillment from a fear-based perspective puts you on a slippery slope, which may start out as overwhelm. Unattended chronic overwhelm can progress quickly to exhaustion, cynicism, and/or powerlessness. When those symptoms become chronic, they can quickly become overextension, disengagement, and/or ineffectiveness. And leaving those states to fester too long can give way to burnout. Eventually burnout affects these areas:

- **Health**—cardiovascular symptoms; mental concerns (especially anxiety and depression); musculoskeletal problems such as back, neck, or shoulder disorders; frequent or lingering common infections (such as cold, flu, or gastroenteritis); inflammatory conditions; type 2 diabetes; weakened immune system; *plus* low physical activity and obesity.

- **A sense of fulfillment and purpose**—depleted capacity for serving others and experiencing happiness and success through your work due to not giving yourself enough experiences to restore a diminished soul.

- **Productivity**—decreased work capacity and innovativeness.

If you're feeling burned out then you probably got there unwittingly. No one actually thinks, "Ya know what would be cool? I'd love to fight uphill battles all day long for the benefit of people I think are unworthy and unappreciative of my efforts—all while dragging my ass—wouldn't that be great!" While *we may not think* we chose this stressed scenario for our life, unconsciously we did.

As I mentioned, employer-provided solutions to help you engage are not the most powerful remedies for burnout stress. We must take our recovery into our own hands.

Remedies for feeling burned out are not necessarily a vacation, a new job, a new boss, or a winning lottery ticket. It's often not even just more sleep!

Burnout recovery and personal well-being are rarely found at your job. Your job is merely the place you show up at every day to practice "your work" in exchange for wages. Your "work" is the vision and mission of your soul, what you ultimately want to enable for others and be valued for in return. Your job is like a gym you go to for about forty hours every week to strengthen your ability to practice "your work." Practicing your work is what enables you to feel engaged, connected to a sense of purpose, and to experience validation that you matter.

When we are already less than engaged, we are primarily present to the vision and mission of our ego—make more money, sleep longer, self-medicate longer, and seek more external justification for what we do, say, want, and believe.

> Your job is where you go every week to strengthen your ability to practice "your work." Practicing your work is what enables you to feel engaged and connected to a sense of purpose and validation that you matter.

It's time to wake up and expand your ability to work and live more consciously. Healing from the dimensions of burnout while strengthening your immunity against burnout are *conscious processes*. The time is here to shift away from what I call *the path to burnout*—which enables your physical, emotional, and spiritual decay—to what I call *the path of purpose*—which enables your physical, emotional, and spiritual consciousness and well-being.

The time is now to notice and take accountability for what we think and feel because we create what we think and feel for ourselves and for the world we live in.

CHAPTER 3

A NEW APPROACH TO WORK

Have I Been Working Hard along the Path to Burnout or the Path of Purpose?

People often think of burnout as simply what happens to you when you work "too hard." Most people use the term "hard work" to mean "dedication" to a job. That might include a willingness to work a lot of hours without sufficient energy, civility, a sense of personal power, or a plan to restore these things. It also certainly requires a skilled ability to ignore anything draining (especially broken relationships and intolerable working conditions) or to consider how others might be affected by their depleted state.

I too believe "hard work" is about dedication; yet when it includes a healthy spirit of dedication to what the work can enable for others as well as for the self, it's actually not *hard* work at all. For those who are flourishing with a sense of well-being, dedication to their work comes naturally.

The magnitude to which we exclude soul care or regard for others from our "making a difference" approach to our job is equal to how much we operate from an ego-heavy, working-hard philosophy. That means working without an understanding of what we have to offer easily, and tolerating what is draining us without a regular practice for soul care and nurturing. It's working in a manner through which we cannot sustain a sense of energy, confidence, power, or peace.

Considering others as well as the self is easier when we balance the ego with a soul-fulfilling approach to work. As a result, it feels more like walking a *path of purpose* versus working hard. Through coaching clients, plus experiencing my own personal journey, I have found that one way burnout becomes a consequence is when there is dedication to being focused on what work enables primarily or only for the self. I call this egocentric approach to work the *Path to Burnout.*

> Operating from an ego-heavy, "working-hard" philosophy means working without an understanding of what we have to offer easily, and tolerating what is draining us without a regular practice for soul-care and nurturing.

The ego isn't badly intentioned. Its work is to protect you, keep you safe, and make sure you benefit whenever possible. It is suspicious of everything—including the soul. When we are egocentric, we smother or cloud our connection with our soul. That leaves us vulnerable to others taking advantage of us in the name of "being a good person," "being loving," "being caring," and so on. The ego does what it believes will enable itself to "look good" to others and therefore be justified to believe about itself. You cannot exist without your ego so don't beat it up or make it wrong. It wants to help you but its delivery can come across as clumsy because its approach is often divisive and built on a foundation of fear. In truth, ego is merely doing its job, which is to be on high alert for how you could be harmed.

The soul's perspective, delivery, and approach is inclusive and love-focused. Its work is to be of service to others. In that pursuit, it seeks to protect and help others while doing what is possible to enable you to serve others as best you can. In return, it believes everything—including you—will be well taken care of. You cannot exist happily, be healthy

> You cannot exist happily, be healthy and vibrant, and experience success without activating your soul. To function at our best (especially at a job), we need to balance our soul and our ego.

and vibrant, and enjoy all the success that is possible for you to experience without activating your soul.

I believe, to function at our best (especially at a job), we need to balance our soul and our ego. The best way to do that is to let the soul drive. When the soul is in charge, it will connect with a sense of purpose, calling, define values, and task the ego with keeping boundaries as defined by the values. Remember, the soul is better at taking care of others as well as of your own soul and ego. The ego can only consider the ego of the self. Often, it isn't very good at actually taking care of itself either, because it's inclined to choose what would look or feel good in the moment. As the ego seeks justification for what the ego desires, the soul seeks validation and nourishment for both the soul and the ego simultaneously. In essence, the ego has you looking outside yourself for relief, reason, motivation, and reward. Contrarily, the soul has you look within yourself for relevance, meaning, authenticity, and a benefit for all. The bottom line is you cannot seek control over your ego. The point is to learn to give up control and instead give the ego a strong soul chauffeur to be healthy. That is how you can enable a co-existence between the soul and the ego as you grow, evolve, and recognize what an energetic, civil, powerful, sense of self is for you.

An alternative to the Path to Burnout is what I call *the Path of Purpose*. It's a more soul-centered approach to work.

How do you know which path you have been following? Consider the degree to which you may be experiencing the three primary symptoms of burnout.

Mental and Physical Exhaustion

1	2	3	4	5	6	7	8	9	10

low exhaustion   high exhaustion

Cynicism

1	2	3	4	5	6	7	8	9	10

low cynicism   high cynicism

Powerlessness

1	2	3	4	5	6	7	8	9	10

low powerlessness   high powerlessness

If you scored twelve or higher, you might consider consulting with top burnout scholars by taking the Maslach Burnout Inventory (MBI) and Areas of Worklife Survey (AWS). MBI is the leading tool to measure burnout. AWS is a tool that determines perceptions that lead to engagement or burnout in the workplace. Either tool can be used in any occupation and when completed together, they measure the degree and contributors of burnout.[10]

The closer you evaluate yourself toward the higher levels of exhaustion, cynicism and powerlessness, the more likely you might be clouding your ability to recognize and pivot to the path of purpose and virtuously handle the rewards of success. Unsustainable or trouble-causing rewards of success come to us with a devotion to only making a frivolous difference for ourself.

In addition, the amount of such rewards will be limited to what we can imagine is possible yet be enough to really feel the pain of the inevitable crash we will surely experience in time (i.e., from a job loss, broken relationship, medical setback, loss of income). This crash will not be punishing, but it will feel that way. It will be as jarring as it needs to be to awaken us to being curious about whether there is an easier and more sustainable path to making a meaningful difference for others as well as for ourselves. The energy of the universe is hoping that the harder our fall, the more likely we will become willing to expand our interest in and capacity for making meaningful differences for others as well as ourselves. The reward for doing so will be an expanded ability to recognize opportunities that can lead to a sense of lasting fulfillment. It will also bring the energy to receive and handle internal and material success beyond what we could have imagined or achieved when we were primarily self-focused. This recognition can be the birth of working with purpose versus working hard toward burnout.

Which Path Are You On?

Let's take a look at the two paths.

The Path to Burnout

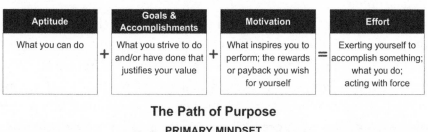

Aptitude		Goals & Accomplishments		Motivation		Effort
What you can do	+	What you strive to do and/or have done that justifies your value	+	What inspires you to perform; the rewards or payback you wish for yourself	=	Exerting yourself to accomplish something; what you do; acting with force

The Path of Purpose
PRIMARY MINDSET

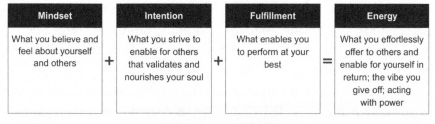

Mindset		Intention		Fulfillment		Energy
What you believe and feel about yourself and others	+	What you strive to enable for others that validates and nourishes your soul	+	What enables you to perform at your best	=	What you effortlessly offer to others and enable for yourself in return; the vibe you give off; acting with power

SECONDARY MINDSET

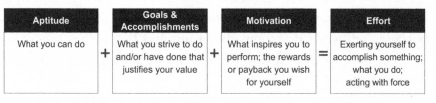

Aptitude		Goals & Accomplishments		Motivation		Effort
What you can do	+	What you strive to do and/or have done that justifies your value	+	What inspires you to perform; the rewards or payback you wish for yourself	=	Exerting yourself to accomplish something; what you do; acting with force

Which path have you habitually followed at work? Contrary to what you might have experienced in the past, you do get to self-select which path to follow. The choice is yours. Let's examine the distinction between the two paths.

Mindset versus Aptitude

Mindset is your attitude. It is a belief of mind, heart, AND soul that gets expressed through what you do, say, and most importantly, through *your being*. It comes through your voice, physique, health, posture, body language, facial expressions, demeanor, and the fashion-adorning way you present yourself. It's a vibe that expresses what you believe is possible—*it's a state of being* that seems to seep out of your pores.

Aptitude is a natural or learned capacity to *do* something. *It's a state of doing.*

It's important to secure an understanding of these two factors because as members of the workforce we often put more emphasis on *what* we do (and can do) over *how* we do it. Yet we all know as consumers *how* we are served matters more than *what* we are served—usually, *how* matters a lot more. Is it any wonder why people of the workforce are more likely to feel depleted more quickly when they strive to be valued more for their aptitude versus their mindset? Frankly, that means so many members of the workforce are like hamsters running on a wheel when they overlook developing and nurturing their mindset.

I believe a big distinction between mindset and aptitude is that mindset *includes* aptitude (what you can do), plus an expanded perspective on making a difference for others as well as for the self. Aptitude alone is insufficient for establishing a connection with a sense of purpose. Yet, when it accompanies a mindset that always seeks *win-win* solutions, a sustainable ability for walking along a path of purpose is not only possible, it is probable.

What does "making a difference" mean to you? How do you feel when you experience moments of "making a difference"? How important is it to you to "make a difference"

1. for yourself?
2. for those you love?
3. for the people and/or causes you serve professionally?

If it were truly possible to make a difference for all three by just focusing on one of these—which would you think is the one you should focus on?

The narrower our scope for making a difference, the harder we will work and the more we will leave ourselves vulnerable for feeling diminished, frustrated, and ultimately powerless. At best, we will experience a false and unsustainable sense of power and stamina because we will experience our power through an ability to win favor from others and tolerate the tough stuff despite being unhappy. You might even convince yourself that fulfillment, happiness, or a connection with a sense of purpose are myths and wanting them makes you weak in some way. We will think our greatest ability lies in getting what we can from others or in being able to read what others want from us and giving it to them. We will give without regard for evaluating whether what they are asking of us will actually get results that matter, or assessing whether we have an ample supply of what we are giving. Our greatest contribution to others is so much more than being strong in our ability to function in debt to the well-being of ourselves or others. When we offer a piece of ourselves we don't have available to give (or expect others to do the same), we turn the person we are serving into a vampire and ourself into their victim.

> When we give a piece of ourselves we don't have available to give (or expect others to do the same), we turn the person we are serving into a vampire and ourself into their victim.

When most people ask us for something, they are usually asking us for their idea of how to achieve something. Rarely do people actually ask for what they want to achieve. Out of fear we listen to the *how* as though it were the *what* and we deliver what others say they want, content to merely cover our ass. *"I did what was asked!"* is often the ultimate defense of those who are aligned with aptitude over mindset and disconnected from their internal power. So when we merely comply with others without seeking to understand, we enable a world of ingrates (them) and martyrs (us).

And vice versa. We sometimes expect of others what they don't have to offer, or we expect others to give us what we want without asking questions. This has no regard for what others may need to accomplish our request, and that way we become the vampire, the ingrate, and they become our victim, a martyr.

Mindset, attitude, or outlook on life comes from the mind, heart, and soul. With that, we can see why a "bad attitude" is so offensive. What's it like for you to be in the presence of someone with a "bad attitude"? It sucks, right? Of course it does, because on a soul level we know we are in the presence of an energy that is not easily changeable. This is someone who is fixed in their mind and heart in a belief that something *bad* is or could happen. They are no doubt bringing a dark past into the innocent present and spewing that out to others. They are holding onto a strongly held belief, either that something bad *could* happen or that they or others don't deserve something good to happen. This is probably based on something bad that happened to them in the past. Yikes!

That's why a "good attitude" is so revered and contagious! When someone has a "good attitude" they are holding onto and projecting a stable, uneasily changed energy that believes in the possibility of benefit for others AND the self, *no matter what happened in the past.* "Good attitudes" are acts of grace. *Grace* means "unmerited favor, love, or help." Who doesn't want to be in the presence of that? That is coming from true power!

Intention versus Goals and Accomplishments

Intention is defined as "the thing that you plan to do or achieve; an aim or purpose." Synonyms include *aspiration, ideal, purpose*. The antonyms include words that imply an aim that is just for individual benefit or gain.

Both *goals* and *accomplishments* are defined as "the ends toward which effort is directed." There's that word again—*effort*. *Goals* are about what you strive to do, to accomplish. *Accomplishments* are about what you have done.

It's important to secure an understanding of these two factors because as members of the workforce we often put more emphasis on what we will do or have done for ourself over what we strive to do or have enabled for others. Often we use our accomplishments merely as a means to demonstrate our value potential to others. The unspoken dialogue is something like this: "Because I did these things in the past, don't you feel safe that I'll likely do them in the future and won't you be lucky to watch me do them!" Self-actualization can only come through understanding how what we can do impacts another. It doesn't come from what we can do for ourself. What we enable for ourself does matter, especially when we are striving for physiological and safety needs. Once our basic needs are met, it's natural to want to feel fulfilled from our work and life. Walking the path of purpose will require our trust that if we regard and focus first on what we enable for others we will align ourself with the same energy and experience validation as well as external rewards effortlessly.

> Walking the path of purpose will require our trust that if we regard and focus first on what we enable for others we will align ourself with the same energy and experience validation as well as external rewards effortlessly.

A distinction between intention on one hand and goals and accomplishments on the other is simple. One comes from a soul-fulfilling approach to work; the other *can* come from an egocentric approach entirely. Often when people talk about their accomplishments, they are talking about amazing things *they* did. When talking about goals, they are talking about what *they* want to do.

All the amazing things *you* did or want to do are not what really make you amazing. Think about it. What makes someone else amazing to you? Most of us are dazzled by people who work toward something bigger than just themselves. That's what intention focuses on. Yet we often give less energy to intention than we do to goals and accomplishments. This is backwards.

The phrase, *"The road to hell is paved with good intentions,"* is distracting and wrong for several reasons. It is often held in the context of what we wish to enable for the self versus the context of what we wish to enable for others. In other words, it's often a goal masquerading as an intention. Another reason this phrase is dysfunctional is that having clarity for our intentions does not mean everything will happen flawlessly. It is true that not all good work has to start with a good intention—sometimes good things are happy accidents. However, connection with a sense of purpose often starts with clarity about what you intend—for others—before regard for benefit to the self. In doing so, we align ourselves with the same intention and, therefore, receive benefit in return.

Goals are not bad. In fact they are necessary to move us forward and keep us in action. Even in job interviews, when people speak of goals or accomplishments, they are speaking about what *they did* and rarely about what *they strived to enable another* to accomplish. Goals and accomplishments are most powerful when they are explained in the context of how they supported a bigger intention beyond benefit to the self. Often we see our goals as *what* we want to accomplish versus what they actually are, which are maps for *how* we will accomplish something meaningful. Goals are much more interesting and meaningful when we

> Goals and accomplishments are most powerful when they are explained in the context of how they supported a bigger intention beyond benefit to the self.

consider how they can benefit others as well as ourselves. Often people just focus on goals or accomplishments without really conveying or understanding the greater intention behind them.

Goals and accomplishments reflect *how* something was done. Keeping the intention in mind, you can convey what the goals and accomplishments enabled for the self *as byproducts* of what was first and foremost enabled for another. Intentions reflect how your contributions have or can make a difference for others, whereas goals reflect a win or a loss; an accomplishment reflects the goal achieved or not achieved. When we have a perspective of others in mind, heart, and soul, then goals become more meaningful and I believe more probable.

Knowing how your work benefits others actually aligns you with vitality, positivity, and power. Your clarity on this reveals something that is unique and authentic about you. This gives you access to feeling validated, useful, essential, and is the enabler of your self-actualization.

For example, people often set goals around losing weight. It is impressive to hear about someone losing weight and how they did it. Yet it's much more powerful to hear about the intention they had for their weight loss, especially when their weight loss affected others. Do you hear the difference in "I wanted to look great at my friend's wedding" versus "I wanted to set a good example of soul care for my kids"? Again, there is nothing wrong with wanting to look great at a wedding, but without the context of how it helps others, it stays as a mere goal or accomplishment. Intention has power and purpose because its potential impact on others as well as the self is clear.

In a work setting, such as at a job interview, intentions share the answer to a question such as, "What can I count on you for, time and time again, no matter what job you're performing or the circumstance you're in?" Intentions share what you want to be valued for enabling for others as well as what you wish to experience for yourself. Getting your mind around the language to explain an intention you hold enables you to explain things about yourself that exhibit the reliability of your character. This will show you as authentically in touch with who you are and your value to the world.

What are the intentions you have for those you serve and collaborate with? How you enable those intentions are where goals come into play. Goals without an understanding of how you can bring benefit to others as well as yourself are egocentric and will require effort on your part to accomplish. Goals with an understanding of how they can bring benefit to others as well as yourself are soul-fulfilling intentions. They naturally open up an energy that can recognize and participate in opportunities that make manifesting your intentions more effortless.

Fulfillment versus Motivation

I define *fulfillment* as "something that satisfies what is required." It's different from *motivation,* which I define as "something that causes a person to act." *Motivation* is derived from words like *content, motive, motif, theme.* These words suggest no change or perpetuity or a recurring pattern with or without a reason for being, doing, or having.

The context of these two factors—fulfillment and motivation—matters because as members of the workforce we often evaluate what there is to get in return for the effort we are expected to put in. So often in my private coaching practice, people tell me that they selected a career path based on what there was to get out of it. They were motivated, for example, by the money, the approval of their family, the ability to have summers off, the job security based on the demand for workers in the profession, and so on. Seeking motivation surrenders internal power to external forces. We know we cannot control what others will offer to us or what the economy will do in the future, yet we favor motivation perhaps because it removes accountability for understanding ourselves.

It is in understanding ourselves that we can experience the full power of who we are, and reward or nurture ourselves in a meaningful way. *Fulfillment* implies something that comes from within or can be met for ourselves by ourselves. Fulfillment comes from connecting to the power within yourself by

- choosing pursuits over outcomes—taking on pursuits to attain the experience of the pursuit while allowing outcomes to be what they will be;
- being open to learning about yourself—observing yourself in action of your pursuits;
- giving yourself support as you journey through a pursuit versus seeking sustenance or justification outside yourself to keep going.

These three activities together enable a true sense of fulfillment. Choosing pursuits disconnects you from the fear of failing. Focusing on the experience of the pursuit lets go of the thought, *What if I go after it and I fail?* Choosing the pursuit instead gives you the freedom to allow a new outcome to emerge. This could be an outcome you maybe never thought of, one that can be even greater than the outcome you originally intended. Fulfillment comes primarily from your actions, while allowing external factors to be secondary. By focusing on fulfillment, we take care of ourselves while we experience a pursuit. The opposite would be finding something outside ourself to feel compelled to stay the course until we get the outcome we desire.

Motivation requires something outside ourselves to compel us to action. Motivation from outside yourself isn't bad. It just isn't more powerful for enabling a successful experience (no matter the outcome) than keeping ourselves fulfilled as we work and go through life. Being open to fulfillment (while we experience a pursuit) opens up our ability to see new opportunities and possibilities. Being open to possibilities is often the energy that success is most attracted to.

To what degree do you typically rely on motivation to come from sources outside yourself for anything you want to accomplish?

Self-motivation is often about giving yourself something you *want* as a reward for achieving something. Often it's a reward in exchange for accomplishing while in debt to yourself.

Pivoting to the path of purpose requires us to pay closer attention to what fulfills us. Motivations are nice, yet we cannot rely on them showing up when we need them. When they do show up, it's okay to take advantage of them. Expressing gratitude for them is essential for welcoming future motivations.

Practicing fulfillment instead is about caring for yourself; it is about giving yourself *what you require* in order to do what you do. Feeling unfulfilled is the call to focus less on what we think others want from us or on what others can and should give to us. Instead, it calls us to focus more on discovering what *we* can offer to others AND what *we can give to ourselves.* Fulfillment offers us the opportunity to control the terms under which we offer our talents and services as well as to feel supported and nurtured when we feel challenged. Soul-care, nurturing, and fulfillment aren't about loving yourself in spite of others. They're about giving yourself what you require in order to do what you do for others. When we don't feel that we will be safe, or have reliable, ongoing access to what fills us up, we often feel like we are not in control, which can lead to feeling vulnerable. Who likes that? We also may be susceptible to constantly trying to fulfill others' expectations, which can be exhausting. That's like living in a messy, rundown hotel room for an extended stay. At some point, you're just *gonna wanna go home*—home as in return to yourself and what fulfills you.

> Soul-care, nurturing, and fulfillment aren't about loving yourself in spite of others. They're about giving yourself what you require in order to do what you do for others.

We must nurture ourselves through challenging situations in order to love ourselves, our work, and anyone or anything else. Giving attention to stress (the corporate-speak word for *fear*), without giving ourselves a counterbalance of energy that feels fulfilling, disconnects us from knowing ourself and being our best. In addition, we disable our ability to discover what we intend for others and to ensure we have what is necessary so we can enable that intention for others and ourselves. In the work environment, it can be easy to make what others think of us be the ultimate permission to feel a sense of credibility and worthiness. If we do this, we are in trouble, because workplaces are filled with people who don't love and accept us—especially when we are not clear about what we intend for *their* well-being.

Focusing on external factors to define whether we are competent, worthy, or even just a good person is the wrong way to go. These external factors could include an admiring boss, backslapping peers, a big paycheck, or an impressive title. Only within ourselves do the answers exist about who we are, what we intend for others, and what fulfills us when we experience something draining. So, relying primarily on external forces or focusing outside ourselves weakens our ability to go within, see ourselves clearly, and work with a sense of purpose.

When you regularly restore your fulfillment tank, you protect yourself from feeling confused, overwhelmed, exhausted, cynical, and/or powerless to get anything done. Instead, you enable yourself to build your decisiveness, responsiveness, energy, confidence, and a sense of personal power—no matter what's happening around you!

Restoring your fulfillment tank happens when you nurture yourself. Nurturing yourself includes being patient with yourself as you discover what fulfills you. It includes practicing making choices for what fulfills you without allowing guilt to steer you away from soul care. Janet Bray Attwood and Chris Attwood, authors of the *New York Times* bestseller, *The Passion Test: The Effortless Path to Discovering Your Life Purpose*, teach their secret that guarantees living a passionate life: "Whenever you're faced with a choice, a decision, or an opportunity, choose in favor of your passions."

That means choosing in favor of what fulfills you.

Sometimes though, we don't get to do what fulfills us. We all know times when the world around us just doesn't seem to be on our side. Emergencies happen, people change their mind, friends and family members need our attention. The world aligning perfectly so that we get what fulfills us all the time isn't what matters most. What matters more for building our energy is the act of discovering what fills us up and then choosing in favor of it. This is an important distinction because it's the discovery of what fills you up and the choosing in favor of it that are *in your control*. They are what build clarity, confidence and a sense of personal power.

> Discovering what fills you up and choosing in favor of it are in your control. That is what builds clarity, confidence and a sense of personal power.

Again, motivation and kind gestures from others can be super helpful and it's fine to accept them. But the clearer you become about what fills your tank, and the more consistently you give it to yourself, the more ready and equipped you will feel to pivot to the path of purpose. The more often you choose in favor of fulfillment, provide it for yourself, and let go of expectations that others will provide it for you, the more passionate you will be about your life. When things work out in your favor, it doesn't mean you identified "good" sources of fulfillment. And, on the contrary, when things work out poorly, it doesn't mean your sources of fulfillment are "off" or that you don't deserve to feel fulfilled. Life and work can be challenging. Sometimes the experiences we face take twists, turns, and a long time to experience fully. We don't need to stop or change our preferences for what feels nurturing and enables our sense of fulfillment. Instead we need to persist and perhaps "up the ante" on what we do in the name of nurturing ourself. The universe is always offering us the experiences we need to evolve.

Practice faith in the energy of your soul to recognize what the universe is putting in front of you and to nurture yourself as you evolve. It's a more powerful, effortless, and stable option than just having faith in the effort of your ego to find motivation.

Energy versus Effort

Do what it takes to operate primarily from energy (and secondarily from effort) to build your confidence and power. I have witnessed and experienced that operating from energy helps in healing confusion, overwhelm, exhaustion, cynicism, and powerlessness. It consciously connects you to what you have to offer and want to experience, versus what you wish to avoid. It stops the cycle of living and working in debt to your well-being.

Energy is the vibe you effortlessly give off to others that reveals your mindset, intention, and level of fulfillment. This vibe is detected by others and often read as your capacity to contribute virtuously to something other than your personal benefit. If your energy seems negative or low, people tend to stay away and think at best that you probably can't handle much more than what you already have going on.

Consider the synonyms for *energy*—they include *aura, chi, ki, vibe, vibration.* These words suggest no effort required. Instead they suggest *the truth of what is.* You cannot fake your energy merely by forcing yourself to do all the things you are supposed to do with a smile. You may think you can, but you cannot.

> Your energetic vibe is a direct reflection of the clarity of your mindset, intention, and sense of fulfillment.

Your energetic vibe is a direct reflection of the clarity of your mindset, intention, and sense of fulfillment. Energy asks, "What do I wish to enable for others?" Energy knows that what it ultimately receives in return will be of similar—if not greater—consequence.

What we often characterize as "bad," "negative," or "low" energy is often the reflection of a dedication to *effort.* Such a vibe reflects someone who values their aptitude, goals, and accomplishments, as well as one who needs motivation. *Effort*—also known as *strength* or *drive* or *stamina*—is exerting yourself to accomplish something.

Effort is a byproduct of energy. Synonyms include *elbow grease, exertion, expenditure, labor pains, sweat,* and *trouble.* These words suggest *a whole lotta* "Whew! This is hard work!" Relying on effort alone requires an external force (muscle, education, skill, credentials, titles, formal authority) to achieve an end. Effort asks, "How will this get done?" In return, it usually seeks a greater return than might be earned by what it gave. Effort without energy leaves you vulnerable to experiencing exhaustion, cynicism, and powerlessness—experience those symptoms for too long and they can lead you to burnout.

People who believe in possibility, grace, and the well-being of others as well as themselves are natural do-ers. There's no such thing as a person with energy who doesn't "do anything." Would you ever view Gandhi as "doing nothing" when he was on a hunger strike for peace? Were John and Yoko "doing nothing" when they didn't leave their beds for one week in the name of peace?

Energy is power! It's contagious and when you have it, people want to be in your presence. They feel their spirit elevate when they interact with you. Energy leads on the path of purpose and effort is a natural byproduct. On the path to burnout, effort leads alone and eventually suffers from a lack of energy.

Egocentric Approach -> Effort -> The Path to Burnout

Being on the path to burnout is a byproduct of a conscious or subconscious egocentric approach to work. What I mean by *egocentric* is being aware or unaware that the concern, or regard

- is primarily or only for the benefit or protection of the self— "What do I want?" or "What's in it for me?" (a.k.a. "WIIFM").

- is focused on thoughts or feelings based in lack or fear—"What don't I want?" or "What don't I have?" or "Something bad might happen if I _____."

- is indifferent to others' concerns or to how what is good for the self might adversely affect another—"That sounds like a whole lotta your problem!"

The Latin term *ego* means *"I."* So when we come from ego, whether intentionally or not, we might come across to others as selfish, negative, needy, whiny, "bratty," and limited. The ego is divisive. It alienates others and tends to cloud access to truth and to its own soul. The ego needs external forces to define itself or give evidence of what's possible. The ego cannot achieve a lasting sense of fulfillment. It is attracted to what feels good in the moment. To create beliefs about itself, it relies on how it interprets what other people appear to do, be, say, or have. A strong ego with a silenced soul cannot take a broader perspective to include others and/or take the greater good into consideration.

So, when we approach work with the ego in the driver's seat, we align with things (aptitude, goals and accomplishments, and motivation) that require our effort. In essence, an egoic approach is at best vulnerable to achieving through pleasing others, protecting itself, or using others. At its worst, it may use manipulation, as well as instilling fear, intimidation, or force upon others. In doing so, egocentric approaches enable for themselves the very same experiences they give off to others, including those they wish to avoid or stop from happening to themselves. For example, when we are mean, we get meanness back from others; when we are deceptive, we often get deceit back from others.

Overall, we risk our connection to a true and sustainable sense of self-clarity, personal power, and purpose when we operate from ego, effort, and the path to burnout. Early in my career, I believed in and followed the Path to Burnout. I believed that success comes more easily when you have some special talent or ability. I believed that my accomplishments and experiences mattered more than what I enabled for others. And I certainly believed something outside myself (motivation for rewards) was more important or meaningful than what I could give myself (fulfillment). I couldn't yet imagine an alternative and if you had spoken about mindset, intention, or fulfillment, I wouldn't have known how to wrap my mind (no less my heart) around those concepts.

I still believe success is possible with the Path to Burnout—it's also exhausting, not fun, unsustainable, and can leave you vulnerable for feeling unfulfilled no matter what or how many material rewards you get in return.

During my many years as an HR executive, I have witnessed countless people in performance counseling become upset about not being valued because of

- what they could do ("No one gives me the chance to utilize my full abilities.").
- what they had already done despite not hitting the intended target ("I do the best I can!").
- being self-motivated ("My boss pays no attention to me and still I get my work done!").
- how hard they work ("I'm working so hard. Why doesn't anyone see or appreciate that?").

How dare other people not see all these wonderful things about me! was the bubble fixated over their head while they were in their performance counseling meeting.

From them I learned that what you do matters, *yet* it is never as important as how you impact *others*. Relying primarily on ability, accomplishments, motivation, and hard work is an attempt to earn success through effort with too little regard for understanding how you wish to impact others, which is the very essence of self-actualization. Other benefits that relying on effort drop by the wayside are developing your internal power and regularly putting any *gas in your gas tank*. This is a setup for aligning yourself with exhaustion, cynicism, and feeling like everything is an uphill battle. With this egoic frame of mind, accomplishment is perceived as possible only when you ignore (or quiet) a full exploration and understanding of who you are, what you actually have to effortlessly offer, and what you want to be valued for in return.

Demonstrating that you have an ability to do something, have the motivation to do it, and are willing to work hard are nice qualities. But let's face it—*nice* isn't always *kind*, meaning *nice* isn't always interested in growth and expansion. *Nice* is pleasing, agreeable, socially acceptable, appropriate. *Kind* is loving, of a helpful nature, gives pleasure, relieves, is attentive, and is considerate. *Nice* doesn't ruffle any feathers, yet *kind* does what is necessary to make a difference. In the workplace, nice makes you a dime a dozen. Your brand of nice doesn't guarantee your value, neither may it align you with what's required for your job nor match the culture and values of the organization or your peers.

On the other hand, people will always value energetic vibes that are healthy, loving, helpful, pleasurable, relieving, attentive, and considerate. Even if you are full of mediocre skills, a so-so work ethic, and are motivated by things that no one else around you can relate to—you will be more valued. Why? Because your mindset matters more to others than your aptitude. The intentions you strive to enable for others make more of a meaningful difference in the world than the accomplishments you might seek for yourself. And the fulfillment you give to yourself is easier to secure and more effective for restoring what has been depleted than the motivators you wait for from others. Overall, others revere and trust what we make look easy to do more so than they revere and trust what we struggle to do. That's the essence of the difference

> The intentions you strive to enable for others make more of a meaningful difference in the world than the accomplishments you might seek for yourself. And the fulfillment you give to yourself is easier to secure and more effective for restoring what has been depleted than the motivators you wait for from others.

between an easy, pleasant-to-be-around energy-fueled vibe versus an effort-fueled vibe.

There may be limited exceptions to this truth. For example, if you have hard-to-find technical skills or specialized knowledge. But requiring that stuff for most jobs isn't the norm and when someone else with all that stuff comes along AND operates from energy versus effort, you'll be out of there as soon as your manager can convince HR and Legal to get rid of you.

Have you settled for understanding what you can or should do, or what you believe others expect of you? Have you tied your self-esteem to something you accomplished or were affiliated with in the past? Have you focused on what *YOU* can get or believe you *need* in order to perform at your job? Did you ever complain when you didn't get what you felt entitled to because of how much effort you put in? Have you worked so hard that you are now exhausted, cynical, and feeling like no matter what you accomplish it's never enough?

If so, why would you settle for that and stay on the Path to Burnout? Could it be because you have become conditioned for the path to burnout?

CHAPTER 4

IF YOU'VE BEEN ON THE PATH TO BURNOUT, IT'S PROBABLY NOT YOUR FAULT

Have You Become Conditioned to Walk the Path to Burnout?

There are two ways we become conditioned to walk the path to burnout.

1. The chase for rewards
2. The fear of not fitting in

Let's look at each.

The Chase for Rewards

One of my favorite authors is David Hawkins, MD, PhD. His book, *Success Is for You: Using Heart-Centered Power Principles for Lasting Abundance and Fulfillment,* starts out with a reminder of an experiment studying a monkey in a cage and its reaction to bananas being placed beyond his reach outside of the cage. If you know this story, you will recall that the monkey struggles to reach the bananas while ignoring an open door on the opposite side of the cage. He struggles so much he even injures himself by trying to squeeze through the bars of the cage.

I see the cage as a metaphor for our job, the monkey as a metaphor for our ego, and the bananas as a metaphor for all the material or external rewards that may come from working: money, fame, a title, respect from others, a reputation, recognition, job security, promotions, skills, knowledge, experience, education. When the ego (the monkey) is in the driver's seat and it is working hard for material or external rewards (bananas), it doesn't easily see any alternatives for getting what it wants or for recognizing opportunities that might in fact be right in front of it. That means, we become the *stop at nothing even if it means harming or killing myself (or others), in the process* monkey; the cage is our job. If we see bananas (ours or anyone else's), we want them. Often for no other reason than *they exist*, which drives a false conclusion that we *should* therefore have them.

What's missing when the ego is in charge is having regard for non-material or internal rewards. These are different than material or external rewards. Internal rewards are the foundation for our ability to fully receive, handle, and enjoy material rewards. Internal rewards include a sense that you are making a meaningful difference for others and in doing so, experiencing a difference being made for yourself. Internal rewards would occur to you as a peaceful willingness or joyous excitement to nurture yourself through experiences that feel challenging or take you outside your comfort zone. Forgiveness for yourself and acceptance of others or situations as they are, while exercising and respecting personal boundaries of yourself and others, happen with compassion and love. Internal rewards such as a feeling of peace, balance, optimism, happiness, energy, openness, confidence, growth, fulfillment, cooperation, and help when you need it are foundational when they are *the norm* in your work and life.

> Internal rewards such as a feeling of peace, balance, optimism, happiness, energy, openness, confidence, growth, fulfillment, cooperation, and help when you need it are foundational when they are *the norm* in your work and life.

Without a foundation of internal rewards, we cannot make meaningful use of the material rewards that come to us without risk of injury or harm to ourselves or others. True happiness, success, engagement at your job, or a connection with purpose are never achieved via struggle. Nor do they carry a risk of reckless injury or harm to the self or others. When we are internally fulfilled, we avoid the biggest temptations of hard work. That means chasing rewards through an uphill battle, exposing ourselves or others to undue risk, and accepting unnecessary collateral damage. I also believe that a more egocentric approach to work finds struggle virtuous and often is annoyed by those who *achieve and receive* with ease. How do you feel about people who seem to achieve with ease and enjoy an abundance of fruits from their labors? Any Tom Brady fans out there?

When you are operating with a solid internal foundation, both non-material and material rewards are merely a byproduct of an ability to see and act on opportunities that are easy for you—and usually right in front of you. You are able to build a solid internal foundation when you surrender to observing yourself over others; accepting and experiencing your thoughts, urges, and feelings; and taking care of yourself through depleting moments to restore your ability to enable meaningful differences for others and yourself in return.

Do you approach your work on the lookout for what others are doing or how they are reacting? Do you ignore or judge versus allow yourself to experience your thoughts, urges, and feelings? Do you actively work to restore your well-being in a productive way when you feel depleted? Do you approach your work on the lookout for opportunities to make a meaningful difference for others?

If you're feeling tired and burned out at the end of the day, or trapped in your job, then you may or may not be in the wrong job—that's for you to know. But I am certain that your ego is in the driver's seat and you are experiencing the side-effects of reaching for "bananas." And when our ego is behind the wheel, we are never authentically equipped to heal from the dimensions of burnout or burnout, no less recognize the path of purpose.

One way I have seen and even personally experienced that we get and stay stuck on the path to burnout is that we seek to receive *bananas* versus seeking to understand and offer *our work*. Remember, "your work" is the intention you wish to enable for those you serve. When we offer "our work," we give ourselves a sense of peace and full confidence that bananas are not just possible, or even probable, but that there is an easier path toward them. We quickly become more and more aware of their presence and develop the ability to receive them without believing we must take on a degree of undue harm or hardship in the process.

Shifting your focus to gain clarity about your mindset, intention, fulfillment, and energy is like the monkey walking through the open door located on the opposite side of the cage and gaining easy, pain-free access to all the bananas it wants. Your true sense of value and self-worth is experienced when you offer what you believe makes a positive impact for others. Shifting to gain clarity about your mindset, intention, and fulfillment builds your energy and enables you the possibility of something else ... happiness!

When we shift our focus, we give up the huge threshold of pain and suffering others are willing to endure in an attempt to get more bananas. Why have we accepted this torturous threshold of pain as we tried to get bananas? Because we made bananas mean more than they are and we falsely believe they have more value if they were hard to get. After all, bananas are just rewards—replace *bananas* with money, material things, as well as promotions, authority, resources. Even though we cannot live by bananas alone, they have falsely become the cause or symbol of success that justifies our right to believe we deserve to be, should be—and it's okay to be—happy.

> Even though we cannot live by bananas alone, they have falsely become the cause or symbol of success that justifies our right to believe we deserve to be, should be—and it's okay to be—happy.

In truth, however, happiness is the cause and bananas are the effect. When we strive for or chase after an effect (bananas), we will expect, accept, and proudly bear a degree of pain and suffering with our job. Over time, this will lead to chronic overwhelm, exhaustion, cynicism, powerlessness, and eventual burnout. Yet, when we strive for internal fulfillment, we have greater access to happiness and the path of purpose. This gives us the capacity to offer our work with ease, energy, and joy. We will have the capacity to experience a sense of accomplishment. We will also have the capacity to receive (and handle) more "bananas" than we can even imagine having over time. Internal fulfillment and happiness are what inevitably leads to a sense of success with no effort required!

Two banana-related quotes from Dr. Hawkins's book are these:

> *Most of the world has gotten just enough of the bananas to permanently trap themselves right where they are.*

> *If we're tired and burned out at the end of the day, then it's from the monkey business of trying to grab the bananas.*

So do you see why enough bananas, sometimes even just one, are enough to keep you stuck and struggling? Because getting just one teaches us that struggle equates with rewards (bananas). And just like that, we become conditioned to walk the path to burnout.

The Fear of Not Fitting In

Do you perceive danger in not fitting in with the status quo? Most of us do; it's primal. It was most likely reinforced by the generations before who had to be focused on safety and survival concerns. Perhaps their life circumstance *was* about survival and that meant fitting in with the pack. Because they loved you and it was what they knew, they taught it to you too. Under the stresses of war, genocide, a depression, and other hard times, it was no doubt a prudent strategy. However, fitting in with the status quo isn't a sustainable approach for feeling connected with purpose.

Here's why.

When we give effort to fitting in, we often don't fit in. In striving to fit in from a place of *effort* we discover the talents and abilities others have and define as valuable. It then requires us to wait on what they will provide to motivate us to develop and deliver the same talents and abilities. The *effort* mentality often shows us the pack that will drain us over time on some level. In striving to "fit in" from a place of *energy* we often discover our own talents and abilities and in offering them, they bring us fulfillment. The *energy* mentality often

> In striving to fit in from a place of energy we often discover our own talents and abilities and they bring us fulfillment.

shows us the pack we share relatedness with effortlessly. People who discover and embrace their uniqueness can more easily offer what they have to offer and, in return, they are often respected and maybe even celebrated.

In the workplace, *fear of not fitting in* often manifests into being experienced by others as a performance problem. When that fear is left to fester, it often leads to termination of employment (a quick one if you're lucky), or endless disabilities and bottomless pits in our stomachs when we think about our job or workplace. But that's nothing because we can heal from all that even though we will probably only repeat the same pattern with another employer.

Here's the real danger of giving effort to a fear of not fitting in—it disconnects us from understanding who we are and what we wish to enable for others and experience for ourselves. That can be harder to heal from because the answers about who we are and what we wish exist only within ourselves. Once we lose the skill of going within, it's hard to bounce back if you don't first admit you've been seeking justification for self-love from all the wrong places. Such as from a job you can love, a boss, admiring peers, happy customers, a big paycheck, a fancy office, or an impressive title—in other words, from places outside of yourself. Time and time again I have witnessed employees turn to strategies to stay secure in the status quo, strategies that unwittingly kept them stuck on the path to burnout.

Strategies that Unwittingly Keep Us on the Path to Burnout

Being focused on bringing protection or benefit to yourself or looking for justification for your sense of self-worth from outside sources are what keep you feeling stuck or in survival mode. When others see us in this mode they might relate to us, but rarely do they admire us because they (probably subconsciously) know this is a depletion of personal power that comes from working from effort. This approach is unconscious living and working and is fueled by trying to avoid feelings of shame, guilt, grief, sadness, and anger. At best, it seeks to experience a sense of pride. Working from the path to burnout perceives an expectation that we must become *strong* to keep giving and giving and giving without boundaries or adequate soul care. Recognizing and acting on a sense to refuel might have us thinking of ourselves as weak or selfish, thereby evoking fear that "our pack" may judge or reject us.

> In the vicious cycle of being externally focused, we fear losing our place among our peers and veer onto the path to burnout.

We might also falsely believe that recharging ourselves can only come from material resources outside ourselves, or from what others give us. When we are primarily aligned with satisfying our ego, we will never recognize an adequate amount of external resources. In response to the void, we blame a lack of resources, the perceived needs of others, and a lack of understanding from others as the reason why success and soul care are not possible. In this vicious cycle of being externally focused, we fear losing our place among our peers and veer onto the path to burnout. Over time, we feel stuck on this path—like an eagle living (and dying) among chickens.

Without a solid internal foundation, understanding what we have to offer, and giving ourselves what fulfills us, we tend to operate primarily from three egocentric work strategies to stay in the good graces of the status quo. We do this in order to experience what we mistakenly believe is a sense of confidence, personal power, and ability to keep pace and peace with our job or life circumstances. Yet these approaches ultimately diminish our soul. We are often painfully aware of our soul diminishing, yet feel powerless to change.

The three egocentric work strategies I have witnessed countless times in the course of my work include

1. pleasing others
2. protecting yourself
3. riding coattails

I have frequently heard people justify that they should be given favor in some way because of how *hard they work*. The truth is what they were usually working hard at was pleasing others, protecting themselves, or riding coattails. Let's look at each.

Pleasing Others

Pleasing others is often a natural byproduct of being focused on offering a soul-centric approach to work. Pleasing others through an ego-centric approach to work is often known as brown-nosing or ass-kissing.

Pleasing others from an ego-centric place becomes a strategy versus allowing it to be a byproduct of true service. It happens when you learn to give what you think you have to give because it's what works for keeping another individual, group, or authority figure happy or off your ass. You may then falsely experience the result as being valued. Believing that you have to give something that you don't have requires you to buy into what people say and think about you. When you focus on only giving others what they want, you become vulnerable for

> Pleasing others as a strategy risks your ability to maintain confidence and dignity, no matter the feedback.

losing your connection with being clarified, confident, and convicted to walk the path of purpose.

Pleasing others as a strategy risks your ability to maintain confidence and dignity if feedback from others is negative or if their ideas are different than yours. If the feedback or belief is good—even worse! Other people's good feedback or regard when you give what you cannot sustain further distorts your ability to recognize your path of purpose. You become vulnerable to believing that what another thinks of you is your truth. It's settling for what another wants of you or sees you to be and that creates a false sense of confidence. It is one that cannot be sustained outside the context of the individual who gave you the feedback. This is also how some people come to "ride coattails" throughout their career.

Protecting Yourself

Another ego-heavy work strategy I have seen many times in my career is protecting yourself. It is called either CYA or WIIFM. CYA—as in Cover Your Ass—means you do your most diligent, thorough work when you keep copious records and evidence to refer to if anyone asks why you did or said whatever you might have done or said. It's not wrong to keep such records. But when you do them *because* you believe others may try to pin any catastrophes big or small on you, such record-keeping often comes from your ego, which is seeking protection, versus from your soul, which seeks to serve.

Are you experiencing the fear of intimidating consequences that may fall upon you should you not measure up to your peers' standards? These standards may be unclear. Or are you concerned about the general *failure isn't an option* tone set by upper management?

Maybe you even witness a few other fear-based affirmations spoken regularly, both seriously and in jest:

- "work smarter, not harder" (translation: you're overlooking something obvious and your hard work isn't enough)
- "shit rolls downhill" (translation: expect shit or shit *will* touch everyone at every level of this company—including you!)
- "the inmates are running the asylum" (translation: dysfunction rules)

We devalue (and eventually deplete) ourselves when we settle for a paycheck in exchange for an opportunity to show a calm, happy face despite experiencing fear of imminent failure, shit, or dysfunction.

With this going on, it's no wonder that at some point in your career you might catch a case of CYA. CYA causes you to listen to everything going on around you through a filter of concern for your own well-being or benefit. With CYA, the ego is in charge. When people are in this mode, they might look as though they're focused on getting all they can for themselves. They justify their behavior with excuses or reasons usually based on their reaction to another's behavior.

CYA asks questions like these:

- "How do I cover my butt if this goes the wrong way?"
- "Why am I in trouble? It wasn't my fault!"

Do you know what WIIFM (pronounced *wiff-em*) is? It's another acronym that stands for What's In It For Me? WIIFM takes CYA one step further in that it's also concerned with what there is to get in return for something it has contributed.

In addition to the questions asked with CYA, WIIFM asks things like these:

- "What do I get out of this?"
- "How is this my problem?"
- "Why should I go out of my way?"
- "Why didn't I get what they got?"

A WIIFM mentality has no understanding of what its soul wants:

- it wants what its ego can get,

- it wants what it can do easily,

- it will prostitute itself for anything if what it can get in return is attractive.

CYA and WIIFM put your power in someone else's control; they are reactive mindsets that operate with the ego in charge.

WIIFM typically reacts to what it receives with more questions such as *Why not more?* or *Why did it take so long to get this?* When questions like these become dominant thought patterns, we start to look for happiness outside ourselves, focusing on external factors for job satisfaction.

People align with CYA and WIIFM work strategies out of fear that they could lose their job, their pay, or their reputation if they don't protect themselves. WIIFM also seeks pain and suffering damages for the pain it's endured. What's implied in this way of working is quid pro quo, which is Latin for "this for that." CYA and WIIFM put your power in someone else's control; they are reactive mindsets that operate with the ego in charge.

Working with ego in charge causes us to measure love and success on and off the job through a filter of *shoulds*. A successful business person *should* have a private jet, expensive cars, exotic vacations, and so on. *If I don't have these, I am not a success. Maybe others will think I am not as successful as I think I am or desire to be.* Those who matter most to someone with the ego in charge are the people who bring benefit to them. An egocentric focus is exhausting AND it's insatiable. No matter what it has, it will never feel like enough. True senses of abundance and fulfillment are byproducts of "offering" acts versus acts of "giving and receiving" or just "giving, giving, giving" or "getting, getting, getting." Its means of taking care of itself is to take breaks from the external forces that cause it pain. Such breaks include time off from work, mid-day naps or binge watching from the sofa, welcoming chaos or distractions into their life, or self-medicating antics. It doesn't think about *healing* the source of its pain.

> Corporate environments can be the ultimate manufacturers of CYA and WIIFM mentalities when they accept results achieved through fear-based values or strategies such as intimidation, bullying, harassment, and do-more-with-less messages.

Corporate environments can be the ultimate manufacturers of CYA and WIIFM mentalities when they accept results achieved through fear-based values or strategies such as intimidation, bullying, harassment, and do-more-with-less messages. Who could blame you for temporary attacks of CYA or WIIFM if you are in a fear-based culture? These conditions are incredibly common and contagious in fear-based work environments. When it's prevalent in the work culture, employees become conditioned to feel content to walk the path to burnout.

Riding Coattails

Another, often subconscious, behavior is called riding coattails. Riding coattails is when someone else who is doing well at their job value what we do for them (for whatever reason—maybe even for a reason we don't fully understand), and we work hard for *their* continued success. The hopeful payoff for this investment is that they will bring us along with them on their career journey. So when they move jobs, we hope they will call us and make us an offer to be on their team at their new employer. We believe their moves and subsequent success dictate our greatest potential for growth and success.

Unwittingly, we live like an entitled child attaching our status and fate to their status and fate, our success to their success, our bonus potential to their bonus potential, our growth to their growth. If they don't do well, retire, get sick, move somewhere we don't want to move, we become stuck.

> When we settle for the power we feel from pleasing others over the power we connect with from offering what's true and easy for us to offer, we are vulnerable to riding other powerful people's coattails.

Fear wells up and we suddenly feel like we have lost our "place," our sense of self, and our optimism for the future. Why? Because we will have to define our potential, value, and worth to another higher-up-the-corporate-ladder stranger where who we are and what we can do may not translate. Any new group of clients, peers, or people in authority is a threat, since it's exhausting to win another's approval. Who would want to "work hard" to do that again?

The truth is, riding coattails is simultaneously pleasing others while protecting yourself. When we settle for the power we feel from pleasing others over the power we connect with from offering what's true and easy for us to offer, we are vulnerable to riding other powerful people's coattails. It can occur when you allow other people to define your value or when you put more value in the perception another has about your value over discovering the value you actually can offer to others.

Riding coattails is risky. Have you ever left a job because a boss who left recruited you to come work for them at their new job? Did you take that job without fully understanding if the new opportunity was a good match for you, your values, and perhaps even with the needs of your family? Are you so loyal to someone at your current job that the thought of them leaving freaks you out professionally? If so, you just might be riding someone else's coattails as a strategy for justifying your value and protecting yourself. It's a wonderful gift to be loyal and believe so much in another and their contribution that you support them. But to do so to the point that you are not sure you could articulate your value proposition to another, do well, or be as happy and secure at your job without that person is not helpful for securing happiness and success. You won't be engaged with your work—you are engaged with a person. It might be a red flag that your primary work strategy may not be to make a meaningful difference, but to ride another's coattails.

Where have you been on the work strategy scale?

←——————————————————————————————————→
-   +

Pleasing Others, Protecting Yourself   Making a Meaningful
and/or Riding Coattails   Difference

It's Never Too Late to Pivot

People who are ego-heavy in their approach to working hard are those
who chase justification for a sense of success and for reasons why they
should *do (versus be)* their best. This is a me-Me-ME way of thinking. We become less than engaged at our jobs (and certainly from our
work) when we struggle with thoughts such as:

> *What do I love to do?* Versus *What would enable me to be and
> offer my best to others?*

> *Where would I love to do it?* Versus *Where are there opportu-
> nities for me to make a difference for others?*

> *Who do I want to work with?* Versus *Who do I share experi-
> ences with and relate to?*

> *What rewards are possible for me to get?* Versus *What differ-
> ence can I make for others?*

"I" and "ME" thinking puts your value proposition in the employer's
hands. So why would they value us if they have to figure out how we
can add value?

How much do you value people in your life who seem to be primarily focused on themselves over anyone or anything else? Being
focused on finding something for ourselves that we believe exists outside ourselves only sets us up for fleeting moments of fulfillment from
our job. An opposite approach would be to figure out what we can do

that makes a difference for others and then seeking opportunities to do it. Thinking you can compartmentalize a selfish focus and contain it at your job while also being a great, loving person outside your job perpetuates a myth. It creates disharmony. A value system in one area of your life is going to spill over into all areas of your life.

When we dedicate our time and effort into an egocentric way of working hard, we are siding with the exact opposite energy of what will connect us with happiness for our work. In doing so, we also block our ability to be energetic, civil, and confident in our ability to accomplish what has meaning for us. We also certainly block our connection to the path of purpose. Consider these beneficial byproducts of having that connection: belonging, energy, positivity, powerfulness, receiving more material rewards than we could imagine, being able to responsibly handle and enjoy more material rewards, and the unveiling that enables you to see your purpose and calling more clearly.

> When the strategies of the path to burnout become the dominant means through which we experience security at our job, we have become conditioned to finding satisfaction and value outside ourselves.

When the strategies of the path to burnout become the dominant means through which we experience security at our job, we have become conditioned to finding satisfaction and value outside ourselves. We think sexy projects, bonuses, recognition, more money, more responsibility, or a kinder, gentler boss will fix what's ailing us. Then, when our external environment doesn't make our pain go away, we think it's time to take an extended vacation, or a stress-related disability leave to try to get a break from our place of work. Eventually that will give way to fantasies of retirement, or getting laid off with a hefty severance package, or we will implode on ourself and think we should switch jobs or even careers to heal from our job trauma.

But no matter how much money we accept, or how many times we switch occupations, industries, companies, or bosses, the egoic way focuses continually on how YOU are being served, protected, or rewarded by forces perceived to be more powerful than yourself. That's letting the ego drive along the path to burnout. And whenever we let the ego drive, we eventually end up crashing. The longer we take an egocentric approach, the longer we experience pain and discomfort at our job and no doubt in life. And we'll eventually head into (and maybe stay stuck in) being less than engaged and even progressing further into job burnout and ultimately depression and other health issues.

If you can relate to getting caught up in an egocentric approach, don't beat yourself up. The good news is you can make a new choice. It's not as hard as you may think (and it's never too late) to pivot to a more soul-fulfilling approach to work and walk the Path of Purpose.

> It's actually harder to progress toward burnout and suffer the consequences than it is to recognize you are in some dimension of burnout and then take care of yourself.

I'm Less than Engaged—What Can I Do About It?

It is very common to experience overwhelm and one or two dimensions of burnout at some point in your career. I believe experiencing burnout or any of its dimensions isn't as much a problem as doing nothing about it. It's actually harder to progress toward burnout and

> Don't give your employer the power to decide whether or not you will experience engagement, fulfillment, and a sense of purpose.

suffer the consequences than it is to see yourself in prolonged overwhelm or some dimension of burnout and then take care of yourself. Having your employer make changes that help you is great. And again, what your employer does will never be more powerful than what you can do for yourself. What you do for yourself keeps you connected with your soul and your internal power. What your employer does and can do feeds the ego. Don't make your well-being your employer's responsibility and give them the power to decide whether or not you will experience engagement, fulfillment, and a sense of purpose. Thankfully, that power is actually yours, not theirs.

So how do you pivot from the path to burnout to the path of purpose? Here's how: make a different choice. Seek to control what's actually in your control. To be engaged and get on the path of purpose you only need to control three things. Fortunately, they are the only things you can easily control at work anyway:

1. What you offer to others (your intentions).
2. The way you offer what you offer to others (your mindset).
3. What you ask of others and give to yourself (your fulfillment).

Our sense of fulfillment comes from how we nurture ourselves while we serve others and that includes what we request from others. We are more likely to get what we request when we leave others free to say yes or no without any repercussion, and when we are clear about how getting what we request can make it easier for us to serve others. How we nurture our sense of fulfillment when feeling overwhelmed can prepare us to awaken an awareness of our intention and mindset. Focusing on our intentions and mindset can easily safeguard us from putting too much focus on the factors we cannot control, which often only move us farther away from our connection with purpose.

Returning to a state of engagement is possible with self-observation and soul care that awaken and restore your soul's authority. Having the soul in charge over the ego enables you to develop the clarity, confidence, and conviction to recognize opportunities that are a match with your talents, values, skills, and ambitions. Employers worth working for tend to recruit, retain, and respond favorably to people with clarity, confidence, and conviction for their work.

Shift your focus for yourself. Here's how:

- develop clarity for and balance between your mindset and your aptitude;
- discover the intentions you have for others and support your ability to offer them through the goals you set. Your accomplishments should be evidence of your dedication to your intentions;
- seek soul-fulfillment while expressing gratitude for external motivation.

Are you ready? You can do it! Let's look more deeply at this alternate path and dispel any concerns you may have about your ability to pivot to the path of purpose.

CHAPTER 5

ARE YOU READY TO PIVOT TO THE PATH OF PURPOSE?

An Alternate Path

Are you ready to follow the Path of Purpose? First I will tell you about the path. Then, in case you could use some guidance to pivot toward it, I will show how to condition and strengthen your ability to recognize it and stay on it versus veering back toward the path to burnout. I will also dispel any myths you may have about why working from the path of purpose might be challenging or impossible.

> The Path of Purpose is about working primarily from Energy: what you effortlessly offer to others and enable for yourself in return; it's the vibe you give off when you act with power.

Remember, the Path of Purpose is about working primarily from *Energy* (what you effortlessly offer to others and enable for yourself in return; the vibe you give off; acting with power), *Effort* is secondary. *Energy* focuses first on:

- **Mindset** (what you believe and feel about yourself and others)

- **Intention** (what you strive to enable that validates and nourishes your soul—what you wish for others)
- **Fulfillment** (what enables you to perform at your best)

Energy focuses second on:

- **Aptitude** (what you can do)
- **Goals and Accomplishments** (what you strive to do and/or have done that justifies your value)
- **Motivation** (what inspires you to perform; the rewards or payback you wish for yourself)

This path is a conscious mind-heart-and-soul-centered way of living and working. In your mind, heart, and soul are the answers for what you virtuously want for yourself and others—your truest intentions. Connecting with intention is like plugging into a socket—BAM! Instant access to energy.

In this purposeful approach, there is no expectation that anything be offered that you don't have readily available to offer and it allows for recharging your energy. Pausing to check in with yourself and recharge is seen as a strength that is admired and emulated by others. Although this path may feel easier, ease is not the point, nor is it a guarantee. You will still face challenges with this path. The difference is you are more likely to experience the energy, patience and tolerance for others, and power to face your challenges and grow from them.

Working with purpose requires no changes in yourself. It is a byproduct of self-clarity and finding appreciation and, dare I say, love for yourself. Richard Rohr is an American author, spiritual writer, and Franciscan friar considered to be one of the most popular spirituality authors and speakers in the world. When he was interviewed by Oprah Winfrey about his book *Immortal Diamond: The Search for Our True Self,* he conveyed that it's natural for love to expand. What

> As you learn to nurture and love yourself, you expand in your capacity to serve and love others.

I see in that statement is that stagnation cannot enable sustainable love or a sense of fulfillment. In addition, learning to nurture and love yourself through challenges may well be the most efficient way of opening up your ability to recognize and pivot to the path of purpose while you restore engagement for your work. As you learn to nurture and love yourself, you expand in your capacity to serve and love others. As you expand in this way, so must everything else in your life expand, including your work.

Expansion enables learning what it is you can be relied upon to deliver to others no matter what. It is offering your reliability time and time again without regard for what is going on around you, whether it is deserved, whether it will be received well, or whether you will get anything in return. In essence, you prepare your capacity to be connected with a sense of purpose and receive the rewards that come with that way of living and working.

When you are on the path of purpose, you are working with purpose. That means you are consciously serving others what you have to offer easily. Working with purpose happens when we learn that our job and those we serve in that job are more like a patient who can be cured by our remedy. *Our* remedy is what we can't help ourself in delivering. That makes you the doctor of your services not the unconscious patient of the circumstances. Chronically contributing what you can be relied upon to provide to others is best described as working consciously. Being able to offer it over and over, despite what's happening around you, comes with courage, practice, and perseverance.

Working with purpose offers its truth, which is a clear understanding of whatever you have an unending supply of to offer to others. You offer it because you believe it can make a difference. Even if another person doesn't value what you have to offer, you often can retain their respect because truth prevails. We all know when we are in the face of someone's truth versus someone's act. Working with purpose is working in a manner whereby we can sustain *pep, patience, power, and peace.* We can do that because we are aware of and advocate for what we value most in order to enable what we enable for others.

Working with purpose has nothing to do with being entitled or lazy. It simply does not settle for conditions it knows will not produce the results it believes can make a difference for another. Working with this possibility for making a meaningful difference enables you to advocate for what makes your work as easy *and probable* as possible. It enables you to know and exercise your boundaries. *To advocate* means to calmly ask for what you value and for what would make a difference in your ability to deliver service to others while fully allowing yourself to have the experience of hearing "no" as the answer. Hearing "no" does not mean it's time to throw down an ultimatum or turn your request into a loud demand: "Give me what I want or I will quit!" Hearing "no" means it's time to side with a new possibility—and a *knowing*—that another solution that will work for everyone involved is around the corner. Advocating is not whining, bullying, or pushing for what you want. When we allow for a "no" answer, people tend to subconsciously read our willingness to give them authentic space to answer in a way that works for them as well as for us. We come across favorably to others. As a result, people tend to experience true advocating as confident and sensible. It inspires the most cooperation and collaboration others have the capacity to offer to others. It enables others to surface their greatest ability to find solutions that will work for everyone to get the best results possible for all.

So how do we get on the path of purpose—and stay there? We must

- acknowledge where we are on the scale between engagement, overwhelm, overextension, disengagement, ineffectiveness, and burnout.
- make a choice to put the soul in charge over the ego. Stop doing what enables the ego to be in charge and start doing what enables the soul to be in charge.

- acknowledge (without allowing), any stories our ego might dream up about why the soul in charge will not work at our job to justify staying stuck on the Path to Burnout.

- become OPEN to engagement and the Path of Purpose by learning and practicing a four step method for soul care (I'll share this method with you in a bit).

- receive (versus chase) the byproducts that come with being on the Path of Purpose.

Acknowledging What I've Been Devoted To

> Burnout is a state of heart and mind signaling us that we have stayed connected to what is stressing us out for too long, and we have overlooked or ignored that we have the power to shift our focus.

Burnout isn't simply a sign that we are tired, cynical, and powerless. It is a state of heart and mind signaling us that we have stayed connected to a clear picture of what is stressing us out for too long, and overlooked or ignored that we have the power to shift our focus. The symptoms such as overwhelm, exhaustion, cynicism, and powerlessness are signals that offer an opportunity to look at what you have *devoted* your attention to. What I mean by *devotion* is love for, dedication to, or enthusiasm for someone or something.

The cause and effect relationship is clear in this quote from *A Course In Miracles*:

> *The result of genuine devotion is inspiration, a word which properly understood is the opposite of fatigue. To be fatigued is to be dis-spirited, but to be inspired is to be in the spirit. To be egocentric is to be dis-spirited, but to be Self-centered in the right sense is to be inspired or in spirit.*
>
> *A Course In Miracles*

devotion (*dedicated from your soul*) —> inspiration

versus

dispirited (dis-spirited) (dedicated from your ego) —> fatigue

To be inspired is to be in *spirit. Dispirited* is to be deprived of hope and disconnected from your spirit—spirit being the seat of your soul—the part of you that cannot ever die and must be nurtured and validated. It is important to take care of both your ego and your soul. Taking care of the ego is insatiable and often excludes the soul. However, taking care of the soul nurtures the ego as well. Primary care must be given to the soul to achieve balance.

There may be things you think you are devoted to, but if a sense of inspiration is not experienced in return, are you truly devoted? Perhaps you are simply justifying the ego and unwittingly diminishing your soul in the process. If the answer isn't clear because you feel unsure about your level of inspiration, then ask yourself, "How engaged, overwhelmed, emotionally and physically tired, cynical, powerless, or burned out do I feel on a regular basis?" The quote on the previous page offers the chance to observe how often we live, searching for inspiration, hoping it will lead to devotion. In truth, it's the other way around.

Engagement and being on the path to purpose is more than the absence of exhaustion, cynicism, and powerlessness. It's a devotion to *seeking opportunities to sustain and even expand* your energy, civility, and personal power. It's a byproduct of a conscious or subconscious soul-fulfilling approach to work.

What I mean by *soul-fulfilling* is being aware or unaware that the concern, or regard,

- is focused primarily on bringing benefit or protection to others and does not accept options that bring benefit to some and less to others—"More to all and less to none!"

- is focused on thoughts or feelings based in abundance, gratitude, and/or hope—"What do I (we) have?" "Something good could (will) happen if _____."

- is coupled with deliberate action that favors a consistent, steady, and more vivid experience of what you value or hope for. It seeks clarity, confidence, and conviction for its work.

- is to serve others through civility, collaboration, inclusion, win-win solutions, interest, meaning, alignment of values—"What matters to all (each) of us?" Or "What's in the best interest of the organization, the mission, the customer?"

We can start to shift to the path of purpose by simply observing, acknowledging, and allowing ourselves to experience where we are—either in engagement (and ready to expand further), or in overwhelm, exhaustion, cynicism, powerlessness, or burnout (and ready to heal).

Putting the Soul in Charge

Shifting to the Path of Purpose means we must stop doing what enables the ego to be in charge and start doing what enables the soul to be in charge. Only when the soul is in charge is the ego also taken care of. With both the soul *and* the ego validated, we achieve a solid foundation of internal well-being. Individual well-being enables collective well-being.

The Latin term, *nobis* means "we" or "us." *Nobiscum Deus* is a Latin phrase that means "God with us." *Us* is not only a reference to *you and me*, but, as I see it, also a reference to the soul and ego *together*. So when we come from the soul, whether we intend to or not, we might come across to others as selfless, positive, powerful, confident, calm, caring, inspiring, trustworthy, thoughtful of others, and/or capable of taking the greater good into consideration. In essence, we have a creator or creative energy coming through us. This means we effortlessly enable more and more vividly in our own life what we appreciate, value, and offer to others. All while never leaving the ego behind. The soul is inclusive. Overall, we assure our connection to a true and sustainable sense of self-clarity, personal power, and purpose when we put our soul in the driver's seat, because the soul does not *need* external forces to define itself or offer evidence of what's possible. When our soul is in charge, we are walking on (and able to stay on) the path of purpose.

Acknowledging where we are provides insight into what would feel nurturing and allow engagement and the path to purpose to persist. If we are in any of the dimensions of burnout, we then unblock insight into what would feel nurturing, allowing healing to happen. This is where the work comes in because, if such insights don't come up immediately, we might be reluctant to persist with observing and nurturing ourselves to allow insights to come over time. How can we feel connected to a great sense of purpose if we don't even know how to take care of ourselves when life feels too boring, stagnant, or overwhelming? Have you become too impatient with yourself, your life or others? Impatience is a form of resistance and a sign you are giving too much energy and attention to your ego and not enough to your soul.

If you are feeling impatient or don't know what you want, then ask yourself three things:

1. "What am I doing that I don't want to do?"
2. "What do I wish to avoid?"
3. "What am I afraid of experiencing?"

When we are unclear, stuck, or confused, most of us can easily answer at least one of those three questions. We can use the clarity of those answers by then asking ourselves a most important question: "What would be the opposite of that? What is the opposite of what I don't want to do, what I wish to avoid, and/or what I am afraid of?"

When we engage with that question, we also let go of any preconceived ideas we have about logical opposites (the opposite of *dog* doesn't
have to be *cat*), limits, boundaries, and what we believe is possible.

Inspiration is a byproduct of devotion. To stay devoted to the path
of purpose, ask yourself questions such as these:

- "What would be the opposite of what I don't want to do, what I wish
  to avoid, and/or what I am afraid of?" The answer is your mindset.

- "How can I take care of myself if I am feeling exhausted, cynical,
  or powerless?" The answer is what gives you fulfillment.

- "What do I wish to enable for others and experience (as well as
  be valued for) in return?" The answer is your intention.

Asking such questions and allowing answers to emerge (over time if
necessary) are initial actions you can take to enable a soul-fulfilling
approach to work, turn off the path to burnout, and pivot toward the
path of purpose.

If You Choose the Path of Purpose, You Must Stop Doing This

The ways you think and feel about your work may be enabling symptoms
of burnout to begin and/or to persist. Taking a soul-fulfilling approach
toward your work starts with acknowledging these feelings and your
corresponding behavior. Otherwise, you may be unwittingly sabotaging
your ability to pivot from the path to burnout to the path of purpose.

During my corporate career as an employee relations executive,
I noticed there are commonalities among engaged, valued employees that transcend organizational types, and individual backgrounds.
These commonalities include *believing* and having confidence that
what they offer to others can have a positive impact. Beyond positive
feedback, recognition, good relationships, or even confidence about
what they can *do*, they also have an innate interest in seeking opportunities to offer their best to others. They do this no matter what they

are up against, and with or without a dangling "carrot," promising a company-given reward.

I also observed commonalities among overwhelmed and less-than-engaged employees. They are primarily focused on what others want, are doing, or could be doing (mostly *for* them). They give themselves permission to feel valued *only* if there is external evidence that they *are* valued (i.e., feedback, recognition, money). These workers would typically give a lot of effort to what restricted their creativity and ability to succeed. I also suspected they weren't taking good care of themselves, since many appeared depleted physically and in spirit.

If you spend more time believing that satisfying others is what defines your value over discovering and offering what you can easily do to make a difference, you are no doubt sabotaging your ability to enable a soul-fulfilling approach to work. In addition, if you spend more time believing in what others can do for you over what you can enable for others, you are again no doubt sabotaging your ability to enable a soul-fulfilling approach to work.

At work, we tend to focus a lot on what others, especially our employer, can do for us. Much information and research has been released about the Gallup employee engagement study, including what employers can do to address burnout. The *Wall Street Journal* published an article by Rachel Feintzeig entitled, "Feeling Burned Out at Work? Join the Club."[11] The article is about how the burnout problem is driving up turnover and health costs for companies. It discusses how companies contribute to burnout by creating cultures with universal factors such as these:

- job uncertainty.

- an expectation that you are always in work mode thanks to technology. This includes being responsible for people and initiatives as they happen in other countries. *Who doesn't love a conference call at 2:00 a.m.?*

- an ever-present "do more with less" expectation.

Although many companies do a lot that enables this epidemic, workers cannot be indignant that their company is just not doing enough to help them heal. No longer can we settle for feeling justified to hold fear-based beliefs such as these:

- *Things will be tough.* Do you feel restricted by lack of support and/or resources?

- *There will be resistance or harsh judgment.* Does it feel like everyone around you believes they know better than you about how to do your job?

- *There's no appreciation anyway.* Besides getting the promotion or pay you deserve, do you struggle to remember the last time someone said, *"Great job!" "Thank you,"* or even just *"Hey, good to see you today"*?

- *Everyone and everything around me is "wrong" and I am "right."* Do you think or say out loud, "If only people would listen to me or do what I am telling them to do"?

- *This place is toxic.* Do you swap negative stories with others, such as these: "She did that to you! Listen to what she did to me!" Or, do you contribute lots of evidence about what is wrong with a situation yet offer few, if any, suggestions on how to make things better?

- *Why bother?* Do you justify your lack of involvement to make anything better due to a sense of futility?

- *Who cares?* Do you justify your lack of involvement to make anything better through a sense of contented indifference, as in, "I don't know."?

- *You started it!* Do you use how others treat you or what's happening around you as justification for what you will do or how you will treat others and yourself?

In fact, fear-based beliefs strengthen our muscle for noticing those very scenarios. Do this long enough and you are well on your way to settling for unsustainable solutions and burnout.

Popular short-term, self-medicating solutions are often part of what sabotages soul-fulfilling approaches to work. How often are you indulging in booze, or the use of prescription or recreational drugs to "get through" your anxiety-ridden days or sleepless nights? Maybe it's more subtle for you. Maybe it's just about comfort foods, which might include the occasional chocolate chip "kookie" (as in non-prescribed edible drugs). These can create unwanted weight gain. Another indulgence, excessive shopping, can get you into an uncomfortable level of debt; overexercising can result in a personal injury, or _____ (*fill in your vice of choice here*) that's resulted in unwanted _____ (*fill in your damage here*).

We all know how it feels to have our confidence shaken, to feel directionless, to be down in the dumps, or to operate with low-grade anger or frustration—terrible! And everyone around us can sense it, no matter how well we think we may be covering it up. The point is this. What unsustainable solution have you been settling for to soothe your job-related stress?

> What unsustainable solution have you been settling for to soothe your job-related stress?

It is true that our work environment can instigate situations that contribute to employee burnout. But have companies single-handedly created these cultures? Or have we collectively manifested this epidemic through our fear-based thoughts, feelings, and behaviors born during times of economic uncertainty? In other words, is the workforce truly a victim of capitalism at its worst or are we powerful creators who still must learn to wake up, hold true to who we are and what we have to offer, and trust that external rewards will follow? Can we learn to value most the opportunity to serve others our knowledge, skills, and talents, *especially* in times of economic uncertainty? Can we learn to do that even in the face of fear-filled leaders who habitually

> If you are feeling overwhelmed, your soul is depleted and you hold the power to restore it. You must let go of any false ideas that it's not in your control to revive and thrive. It is primarily in your control.

pass a burden of giving more and receiving less onto their most valued commodity—their human resources?

Now hear this, people of the workforce: If you are feeling overwhelmed, less than engaged, or burned out, your soul is depleted and you hold the most power to restore it. You must let go of any false ideas that it's not in your control to revive and thrive. Actually, it's primarily in your control. Companies make amends with solutions *their* fears will allow—such as recognition and reward programs, periodic pizza lunches, crazy shirt days, bring your pet to work policies, soft-skills training and development, benefits such as vacation time or sabbatical leaves, on-site gyms, and yoga or meditation at work. I'm not trashing any of these offerings. Anything your company offers to provide an environment of fun and to restore your energy matters. They are great win-win gestures that can help employees expand their creative abilities and sense of fulfillment while enabling the company to improve its productivity. And we all know they are not enough.

Recent Gallup reports show that several factors are among key drivers that help employees engage.[12]

- feedback and ongoing communication
- understanding where an organization is and where it's headed (ideally within the next three years)
- clarified expectations including the resources to deliver on those expectations
- opportunities for employees to do what they do best
- hybrid work arrangements where there is flexibility to work from home and the office

- employees feeling that their overall well-being matters and is cared about
- managers who are engaged and set a tone of engagement for employees

Is it any surprise that what these things have in common is that they provide opportunities to experience making a meaningful impact for others as well as for ourselves? Since the engagement numbers reported by Gallup don't seem to change much based on what employers do, could the real power to turn around these statistics be within ourselves?

Instead, Start Doing This

To prepare yourself for the path of purpose, you must start to develop your muscle for *the three C's for a soul-fulfilling approach to work*: clarity, confidence, and conviction.

Clarity

Clarity is *understanding* yourself—knowing what easily enables you to do what you do for others. This includes soul care and a willingness to engage in personal observation and self-discovery.

Confidence

Confidence is *owning* yourself—being consciously aware and certain of your power to enable meaningful possibilities for others. It's *self-faith* that you will act in a *right* way, no matter what the situation. *Right* means the way will be in alignment with the truth of who you are—your personality, interests, talents, knowledge, skills, abilities, and experience. Confidence also knows and exercises its personal and professional boundaries while in service to others. Confidence is a natural byproduct of clarity.

Conviction

Conviction is *offering* yourself—rather than what you think others want from you. The energy to offer what you have follows naturally from confidence. No need for twelve hours of sleep or power drinks. The energy to offer your services requires no physical effort at all. In fact it's the easiest of the three C's. Conviction happily seeks opportunities to do what it does most easily. It accepts the end result as it is without making it mean anything about itself or others. Power comes from offering what we have to offer; not from getting what we can get or from having our offer received or revered. We don't always have control over what we get; we always have control over what we offer. Conviction is a natural byproduct of confidence.

A sustainable ability to be engaged in your work and life and to experience a connection to a sense of purpose are possible through clarity—understanding yourself. Confidence and conviction follow clarity naturally. Our energy and ability to achieve clarity are created when we pay attention to discovering and developing the three things that put us on the path of purpose:

1. **intention:** what we offer others; what you want to enable for others and be valued for in return

2. **mindset:** the context in which we think and behave when we offer what we offer to others; your state of mind

3. **fulfillment:** what we ask of others and give to ourselves; what enables you to do what you do for others

These three aspects determine your *energy*, the vibe you give off to others. No more working from *effort* alone!

You work soley, versus soul-ly ;-), from *effort* when any one of the three components of *energy* is low because your capacity for self-clarity (followed by confidence and conviction) is compromised. When your self-clarity is compromised, your ability to take a soul-fulfilling approach to work and to stay connected to the path of purpose is nearly impossible. An ability to observe and nurture the self is vital for opening up your ability to restore your energy and sense of personal clarity.

Without a skill for self-observation and soul-nurturance, we cannot recognize our connection with a sense of purpose. That's right—*recognize* our connection. We are never disconnected from our purpose, yet when we are less than engaged at our job, it might feel as though we are. When you feel clarity, confidence, and conviction for your work, you can be sure that you are equipped to discover the soul-centric aspects (intention, mindset, and fulfillment), and be aligned with the path of purpose.

> When you feel clarity, confidence, and conviction for your work, you can be sure that you are equipped to discover what will be soul-fulfilling and align you with the path of purpose.

Beliefs that Block the Path of Purpose

The Path of Purpose requires us to acknowledge beliefs we have or stories our ego might dream up about why the soul in charge will not work at our job. The ego strives to justify staying stuck on the Path to Burnout. The biggest roadblock I have seen people encounter on the way to the path of purpose is an inability to understand how to make a meaningful difference for others.

Do you understand what you do that makes a difference for others?

Do you feel like you make a difference for others every day?

Do you feel like you make a difference with every interaction you have?

I believe that deep down everyone wants to make a difference and contribute to others in a way that they believe can make a meaningful difference. This is what it means to be a self-actualized human. And those who say that making a difference to others doesn't matter to them

> Deep down everyone wants to make a difference and contribute to others in a way that they believe can make a meaningful difference. This is what it means to be a self-actualized human.

are probably locked in pain. That pain might come from the challenges of having an emotional or anti-social disorder. More likely it's because they haven't yet set a stable foundation of resources as described by Maslow's hierarchy of needs—physical needs, safety needs, belonging and love, and esteem. As a result, they are blocked from seeing their path of purpose. In addition, they may have falsely accepted that they are powerless to change things they feel stuck about.

So most likely, believing that it doesn't matter to make a difference for others happens for these reasons:

1. **They can't figure out how they make a difference**—they don't believe they can connect to a sense of themselves that could actually matter to another.

2. **They worry that they will have to give "too much" in order to make a difference**—they fear they will be vulnerable for giving something they are not sure they can recover from or sustain giving.

3. **They believe others have the power and control their ability to make a difference**—they believe their ability to do "more" is, or will be, blocked because the people around them won't, or don't, recognize their potential and give them an opportunity or a higher level of responsibility to contribute in a way they want to contribute.

Since you are reading this book, I doubt you are disinterested in or incapable of making a meaningful difference for others or working with a sense of purpose. Yet, if you feel stuck in the pain of burnout and are skeptical about the possibility of being able to pivot to the path of purpose, let's look at each of these possible reasons and dispel their influence on you.

I Can't Figure Out How I Make a Difference

By nature of being human, we are each capable of making a difference beyond just taking care of ourself and our own needs. However, until we learn how to observe and nurture ourselves through challenges, we cannot nurture others in meaningful ways and enjoy a sense of fulfillment. Each of us is born with the wiring that is required to make a meaningful contribution to another. No matter how much someone else may have told us our "greatness" is unlikely, we can erase that faulty programming. We can reconnect to our natural ability to impact others in a way that has meaning for us and thereby feel validation for our existence on this planet.

People often have only a fleeting sense of an innate connection to purpose. Often it is distorted and seems to occur to most as wanting "more" from their job. This might manifest as wanting to be more successful, to be a higher-level leader, or to earn a lot more money. Having that kind of material stuff or recognition is falsely believed to be the secret to feeling satisfied and fulfilled. But it only feeds the ego. When you decide to obtain a deeper knowledge of something you are interested in, can do well at naturally, and can offer to another, you will discover what your connection to purpose is. It's just a matter of time and it can be no other way. It is our birthright as humans to know what we can do easily to serve others, and to have a sixth sense for knowing how to do what we do despite what is happening around us.

> It is our birthright as humans to know what we can do easily to serve others, and to have a sixth sense for knowing how to do what we do despite what is happening around us.

In a bit I will introduce you to a method I have created. This method is a way to start observing and learning about yourself. Self-observation is key for being on the path of purpose and working in a way that we know we make a meaningful difference for others—and ourselves in return. In working from the path to burnout, we tend to focus on *how* we do things. In working from the path of purpose, we tend to focus on *what* we enable for others.

Corporations especially value *how* answers and I believe they have inadvertently conditioned their workers to value themselves based on their capacity to generate *how* answers. *How* answers are appropriate to seek in well-defined *what* situations, such as corporations who know what they are selling or being an expert at something. Yet focusing primarily on *how* doesn't work when it comes to accomplishing something you don't have experience with such as recovering a lost sense of connection to purpose.

For a sense of purpose and fulfillment from your work, you must claim control over *what* and *why* and give up control over all the other stuff. Clouding up your thinking and feelings with things you cannot always control—like *who, when, where* and especially *how*—gunks up the physics of anything you want to create or experience. How could this be?

At our jobs, it's simply not enough to share a vision or to set goals. The demand from your employer for *how* you will make a vision or goal happen is big. Delivering the results you promise is just not enough. They must also manifest the way you said they would. In this way, we erroneously tend to apply the appropriateness of that expertise for our jobs onto ourselves even when we set out to do something we have never done before. So not only do we become married to our *how* plans, we may judge our results and only label them as valid or successful if the results manifest within the well-thought-out parameters of our initial *how* plans.

So in other words we perceive pressure (by ourselves and sometimes others) to predict and control things such as these:

- *how* events will transpire
- *how* people will behave
- *how* resources will become available

It all seems ridiculous, doesn't it? Not only are we limited in how much control we can ever have over events, people, and resources but our initial *how* thoughts are also severely *gunked up*. This happens especially if we are not an expert in the matter at hand.

Here's what I mean. Anytime we try to imagine *how* anything will get done, we immediately think in past tense. Our *how* ideas exist in the realm of what we think is possible based on *how* things happened for us or others in the past. So we believe that's what's possible for us in the future. Again, this might be appropriate in a situation we have a lot of experience in, such as at our jobs.

So what's the right measure of value for *how* versus *what*? Well, there is no *right* answer. There is only *your* answer. In any process or situation, explore the value you have for both your *what* and your *how*. Just ask yourself, *Am I open to some kind of a process, confident of a specific reward? Or am I open to some kind of a reward, confident of a specific process?*

In other words, are you willing to accept various ways in which your *what* could be achieved? Or are you determined to have the process (the *how*) be a certain way, even if it means a different reward? The fastest, most ideal path to your *what* may be very different than your initial *how* ideas.

Certainly for some tasks or life ambitions, it may make perfect sense to hold onto your *how* ideas as well. Even so, the fact doesn't change that the more you choose to value *how* over *what*, the more you put yourself at risk for feeling that you won't get *what* you want if your process isn't unfolding *the way* you thought it should. When things don't happen as you imagine them, you might question the *possibility* of your *what* entirely. You might even question yourself, which will threaten your self-esteem, clarity, confidence, and ability to feel engaged.

Working from the Path to Burnout Focuses on *How*

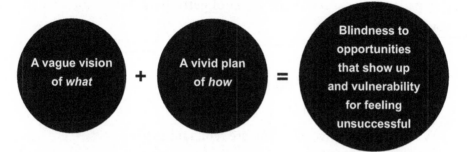

Working from the Path of Purpose Focuses on *What*

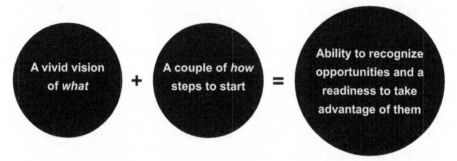

Working with purpose and engagement means setting yourself up to be an expert. Part of what makes someone an expert is that they know how to capitalize on a situation, whether good or bad. That means believing that opportunities exist even in seemingly bad situations and trusting that you have the ability to recognize and act on those opportunities when they do show up. Until an expert clearly sees opportunities that can bring velocity to their vision fully manifesting, they start brainstorming and acting on baby-step ideas to kick-start their opportunity-recognizing energy.

Clarity about what we want and persistence in taking advantage of opportunities to experience what we want is what assures a sense of power and a connection to a sense of purpose.

What If I Have to Give Too Much in Order to Make a Difference?

When you work with purpose you understand the difference between giving and offering. If you relate to believing that serving others will somehow be at your expense, then understand that that particular belief comes from a fear of getting into a situation where you will be

- taken advantage of,
- expected to be what you are not,
- expected to do what you can't do, and/or
- expected to give what you are reluctant to give.

No one likes to feel vulnerable in such ways. Offering has nothing to do with giving people something you don't have to give or want to give.

The universe only gives one response to what we think, have an urge to do, or to what we feel, which is "You're right! Let me show you more!" Thus, I do not endorse adopting or cultivating a belief that requires you to change yourself, others, or your situation to connect to a sense of being able to make a difference. Instead, I favor realizing an opportunity to wake up to something that already exists but might be dormant within you. That something is who you already are and what you already have to offer—no matter what. A willingness to wake up to it is all you need. That willingness will allow you to eventually discover what it is you have to offer so you can make the choice to live and act from it, time and time again, no matter what is happening around you. As a client of mine once said, "It's just an easier way to live and work."

> The universe only gives one response to what we think: "You're right! Let me show you more!"

What if I Believe Others Have the Power and Control My Ability to Make a Difference?

Believing that unleashing your greatest potential is in the hands of someone else puts you on a fast-track to feeling stuck and unsure that you have the ability to make a difference. Why? Because it creates an illusion that you have no internal power.

If you are not sure if you hold this belief, ask yourself these questions:

- How easily can I articulate what I wish for others?
- How do I most reliably function in order to enable that wish?
- Does someone have to give me the permission, authority, resources, and rewards that will enable me (or justify me) to give my best?

I know those may not be easy questions to answer honestly but I assure you the answers are available to you as soon as you decide to take back your power to engage.

> You don't need what you don't use.

The magnitude to which we perceive power to be in the hands of another is equal to how powerfully connected we can feel to what it is we wish for others. It is also equal to how much we trust our ability to consistently contribute to enabling that wish. Simply put, you don't need what you don't use. When you surrender to discovering that wish, how to enable it will become clear if you stay persistent in the choice and decision to discover it. When the answer to how to enable it becomes clear and you offer it regardless of how others behave, you will have instantly made a difference. You must then stay aligned with a belief that things can work out the way they need to work out. When you know you can make a difference, even just by the thoughts and feelings you hold, you keep your power. Then certainly how you feel about your life and experience the conditions around you will change.

Pivot to the Path of Purpose

Burnout is often a result of being fundamentally disconnected from a soul-fulfilling approach to work. That means the ego has been driving and has diminished, perhaps disconnected, the soul. To rectify this, become *OPEN*.

Let's take a look at four steps that can help you strengthen your ability to stay grounded in a more soul-centered approach to work and get you ready for experiencing sustained engagement and the path of purpose. I offer my simple four-step process to *open* the Path of Purpose—the OPEN Method.

It will help you start strengthening your ability to observe and nurture yourself so that you can more easily connect to a sense of purpose and love for your work. It will especially work if you are feeling overwhelmed, confused, stuck, detached from a sense of purpose, less than engaged, or burned out.

Step 1—O for Observe

Acknowledge what you are observing externally and how that observation affects your thoughts, urges, and feelings (mind, body, and soul). Observe yourself in the situation versus judging what others are doing. Learn to discover signs that you are depleted.

Step 2—P for Pause

Practice non-judgment for your thoughts, urges, and feelings. Think what you think and feel what you feel without taking action—just yet.

Step 3—E for Engage

Figure out what will nurture your soul and therefore your ego too. Practice patience with yourself as you figure out how to nurture and support yourself. Practice non-judgment for a depleting experience and for a need to fill yourself back up. Decide what will fill you up. Choose clarity of what you want versus what you don't want. Practice non-judgment and release guilt for welcoming the fulfillment that enables you to do what you do for others.

Step 4—N for Nurture

Take action on what you determine will help to restore you. Practice non-judgment and release any possible guilt for investing time, energy, and resources in what nurtures you. Allow clarity, confidence, and conviction for your work and life to surface naturally.

The OPEN Method is a remedy for effort-filled thoughts, urges, and feelings that might cause you to want to push through tiredness, cynicism, and powerlessness. In the past, you might have wanted to wallow in your efforts and use them as justification for inaction or for turning to vices for comfort. We have to stop using how others treat us or what's happening around us as justification for what we will do or how we will treat ourselves. We must learn how to find, build, and restore our internal source of power.

> We must learn how to find, build, and restore our internal source of power.

Notice that each step builds off observation, which demands no action. Each step builds by letting go of judgment for yourself (which releases guilt) and for others (which safeguards against allowing others to drain you). The OPEN Method is about nurturing yourself versus seeking nurturing from outside yourself—from others or from things. We must stop seeking energy outside ourselves.

The OPEN Method is about gaining power *because* we give nurturing care to ourselves versus seeking anything externally. The thing we actually do is not where power comes from. For example, lighting a candle is one of the simplest things I do to nurture myself sometimes. It's not the candle that holds the power for nurturing me. It's the act of lighting it for myself. The time it takes to remember to take care of myself and do it is what matters. For me, a lit candle is always nice to have in any room I am in, especially when I am facing a task that might drain me or consume my attention and focus. Having someone else light a candle for me is nice and I appreciate it. But when I take the time to light it for myself, it reminds me that I am acknowledging how a situation might affect me and assuring myself that I will be cared for while I face that situation. It holds a different meaning when I do it for myself.

Let's look at each step of the OPEN Method in the coming chapters.

CHAPTER 6

STEP 1—OBSERVE FOR THE O IN OPEN

*Yesterday I was clever, so I wanted to change the world. Today
I am wise, so I am changing myself.*

Rumi

Observe Your Thoughts, Urges, and Feelings

Are you done ignoring, accepting, or pushing through your feelings of overwhelm, tiredness, cynicism, and powerlessness? The OPEN Method is an easy, doable way of restoring your power. You can do this in the regular course of your day—it takes no extra effort. No outfit change, no equipment to drag out of storage, and no lactic acid stiffness to endure while you condition yourself to this practice.

I first came across the value of this outlook and practice from an urge for a cigarette—I will share that story with you in the next chapter. The truth is, I stumbled on this practice. It became my secret way of taking care of myself when I felt triggered, derailed, drained, depleted, stuck, or blah. In other words, whenever I felt any way that was counter to how I chose to feel—calm, clear, confident, connected, focused, productive, inspired, energetic, and optimistic—I did this. The short- and longer-term effects of this practice were beyond what I could have imagined—I just wanted the pain of feeling derailed or depleted to go away ASAP. With this secret practice of mine, they did just that—they went away.

Since then, I have heard of similar methods that enlightened me as to why my practice worked for me and later for my clients. These include the letting go technique by Dr. David Hawkins; *Nature's Guidance System* from Janet and Chris Attwood; and somatic psychology.

The practice for me begins with Step 1—Observe. When something happens that triggers me—meaning overcome by thoughts, urges, and feelings that are counter to what I would want to experience—I Observe. Those thoughts, urges, and feelings might occur to me as experiences such as being vulnerable, sad, disappointed, overwhelmed, helpless, stuck, confused, detached, drained, frustrated, impatient, angry, stressed, guilty. These experiences are built on a foundation of believing something *bad* could happen.

From experiencing such thoughts, urges, or feelings, I ask myself an initial question.

1. *"Am I okay?"*

My answers are typically either yes, no, or not really.

> When I observe that something triggers me, I ask myself, "Am I okay?" and wait for an answer.

My response to *yes* is to move forward. If I am okay I know I am still open and aligned with a sense of clarity, confidence, and conviction to find win-win solutions despite a moment of feeling jarred. My response to *no* and *not really* is to have an internal dialogue through my OPEN Method. I do that by asking myself my second, third and fourth questions:

2. *What do I Observe is happening and what am **I thinking** about it right now?*

3. *What do I Observe is happening and what am **I having an urge to do or say** about it right now?*

4. *What do I Observe is happening and what am I **feeling** about it right now?*

In this step, you focus on Observing yourself by asking the four questions versus judging others or analyzing the situation. The point is to seek truth about yourself (never about others) in order to surface insight into how to effectively take care of yourself beyond basic hygiene (washing, dressing) and health (eating right, exercising, sleeping, hydrating). In nurturing yourself through your depleting thoughts, urges, and feelings, you restore your soul to the driver's seat while calming and assuring your ego that you will get through your depleting experience. Not only will you get through it, but you have a boost of velocity to grow and be ushered more quickly to a more vivid experience of what you want from your job, work, or life. In this practice, you become stronger in recognizing opportunities and enabling productive solutions to surface naturally.

To observe is to notice what you are thinking and feeling in mind, body, and soul without guilt or judgment of self or others. In doing so, you enable yourself to more quickly transcend the hold that the situation, other people, or your own self-sabotaging gut reactions may have on you.

What you will Observe by asking the four questions are three things:

- **Your Mind**—notice what's coming from your head. What do your thoughts say about what's happening? As you experience the situation you are in, Observe *your* thoughts about the situation, others, and yourself. What you Observe is not *the* truth—it's *your* truth.

- **Your Body**—notice what's coming from your body. Is there an urge for a fight, flight, freeze reaction or even a *face it* response? What do you have an urge to do or say based on what you are experiencing both externally and internally? Where in your body do you feel that urge for a fight, flight, freeze reaction or a face it response?

- **Your Soul**—notice what's coming from your heart. What feelings come up for you based on what you are experiencing both externally and internally? What would you rather feel? What do you perceive is stopping you from what you would rather feel? What would enable you to experience what you would rather feel?

When we move into Observation mode, we keep the soul in the driver's seat. With the soul still in control, we can more clearly notice and register what's happening, without allowing the driver's seat to be filled by an ego with a triggered need for control, judgment, protection, or vengeful emotional reaction. Observing merely asks us to primarily notice what we perceive about ourselves until we can productively face others and the situation we are experiencing. It asks us to notice how our perception affects us internally. In this step, we are choosing to face ourselves, others, and the situation by doing what it will take to surface a productive response and move past our initial fight, flight, or freeze reaction without guilt or judgment.

> When we move into Observation mode, we keep the soul in the driver's seat. With the soul still in control, we can more clearly notice and register what's happening, without allowing the driver's seat to be filled by an ego with a triggered need for control, judgment, protection, or vengeful emotional reaction.

Observing and acknowledging what we perceive about ourselves, the situation, and the people around us show us how we might become vulnerable to believing that power is out of our control. When we begin believing in that versus merely Observing our perceptions, we diminish our power. Suddenly power seems to be outside ourselves, and because of that we might feel further triggered as evidenced by feelings such as vulnerability, sadness, disappointment, overwhelm, helplessness, anger, and confusion. Feeling triggered is often a sign that you are coming from an egocentric place. For example, if your boss is yelling and you have unhealed trauma from the past around being in the presence of someone yelling, you are not even in the present moment. More likely, you are feeling an emotion like shame, anger, or shock from the past and the trauma may be deeper than you think.

Whether or not the ego is on high alert from unhealed trauma or not, it can only notice evidence that what it thinks and feels is right for itself. The ego then believes it is justified to take reactive action even if it is unproductive or detrimental to the situation, others, or itself.

The power of Observing is that it enables you to face an understanding of what you perceive internally about yourself based on what's happening around you. Is the yelling triggering memories of unhealed trauma from the past or are you merely annoyed that the behavior is stalling camaraderie and productivity? Taking time to Observe yourself brings you clarity about yourself; clarity is key for pivoting to purpose over burnout.

> The only goal of step one is to Observe what you think, have an urge to do or say, and feel within your mind, body, and soul, without responding.

So the only goal of step one is to Observe what you think, have an urge to do or say, and feel within your mind, body, and soul, without giving in to reactive urges. When there is no pressure to react or respond, there is a lightness and a greater sense of openness to seeing the truth about yourself. You feel better equipped to let go of a need to place blame or judgement on or outside yourself. You open up your ability to simply be with what is and trust that win-win solutions will surface.

In Observation mode, we strengthen our soul awareness. Soul awareness is simply becoming aware of our thoughts, urges, behaviors, and feelings relative to what is happening around and within. Soul awareness is a benefit of developing our Observation strength that comes over time. It opens up our capacity to learn about and care for ourself so that we can evolve into someone who feels ready to learn about and care for people or things with a soul-fulfilling approach.

Developing a soul-fulfilling approach to work is a process like anything else and I believe it is necessary for preventing or healing from lack of engagement and burnout as well as for feeling a connection to a sense of purpose.

When you can acknowledge what is, you also might find it easier to let go of any preconceived notions of what you or others should be, do, think, or feel. In this step you simply ask yourself the four questions (and ask them several times if necessary), until you get clear about what you think, have an urge to do or say, and feel. You know that you are not on the hook to get at *the* truth about the situation or about others. Rather you are on the hook to get at *your* truth about yourself. When you get at and own your personal truth, you can more easily surrender to a readiness to experience what there is to experience from the situation, other people and especially from what you think, have an urge to do or say, and feel.

We are not our experiences. We are *enablers* of experiences. Allowing what might be tough, painful, or depleting experiences is vital for our growth, the evolution of our consciousness, and our

> We are not our experiences. We are enablers of experiences.

capacity to make meaningful differences for ourself and others. It's also vital for our ability to prudently handle the material rewards that come with making meaningful differences in the world.

We can also learn a lot about Observing ourselves from the eagle living with chickens story I shared at the beginning of this book. If you remember, the eagle who was raised by chickens has his attention captivated by the eagles soaring in the sky above. This is something the other chickens around him don't pay much attention to. Noticing what captivates your attention is another opportunity to Observe the thoughts, urges, and feelings that arise from what you are noticing. Noticing does not require you to psychoanalyze why your attention has been captivated. You do not even have to go off and journal about it. Just notice it. Just noticing is an opportunity to have an experience.

Susan David, PhD, is a psychologist who writes and speaks about emotional agility. In her book *Emotional Agility: Get Unstuck, Embrace Change, and Thrive in Work and Life*, Dr. David explains that emotional agility is a critical skill for experiencing resilience when facing change, complexity, or challenging times. She writes that starting your Observation statement with *"I notice ... "* removes the danger of confusing your identity with your thought, urge, or feeling.

For example, for the four questions, respond with "I notice":

Question 1: *Am I okay?*

Answer: "I notice I am ...." Are your answers pleasing to you? If not, it's time to ask the next three questions.

Question 2: *What do I Observe is happening and what am I* thinking *about it right now?*

Answer: "I notice that I am thinking ...."

Question 3: *What do I Observe is happening and what am I* having an urge to do or say *about it right now?*

Answer: "I notice that I have an urge to (do or say what?) ...."

Question 4: *What do I Observe is happening and what am I* feeling *about it right now?*

Answer: "I notice that I am feeling ...."

I find the simplicity of *"I notice ... "* to be genius. Answering the four questions with "I notice ..." establishes a personal identity boundary between your soul and any detrimental thoughts, urges, and feelings. This is important because when you are facing a threat or a challenge that brings up a belief that something *bad* could happen, what you notice is no doubt coming

> Answering the four questions with "I notice ..." establishes a personal identity boundary between your soul and any detrimental thoughts, urges, and feelings.

from your ego. Dr. David reminds us that feelings are not good or bad. Instead she suggests that they are merely what she calls "signposts," giving us clues about our emotional response to what's happening around us. I also believe they are signposts about who is in the driver's seat—the soul or the ego.

When I notice my ego popping up and having trouble settling down, I usually have an internal dialogue with it. I say, *Hold on, my ego. I know you want to protect me. Thank you for that. I'm going to invite my soul in so that as I move forward with a decision to experience such-and-such, you, my soul, the situation, and other people involved will all be taken care of.* This step is about talking kindly to all aspects of yourself.

Kristin Neff, PhD, is the author of *Self-Compassion: The Proven Power of Being Kind to Yourself.* Through her book, Dr. Neff provides evidence about the value of speaking kindly to yourself as a means to heal PTSD and other traumas.

In step 1, Observe, we simply honor what is so for us. This allows the OPEN Method to further unfold so that we stay aligned with a curiosity about ourselves—mind, body, and soul—as well as about others and the situation we are experiencing. Denying yourself step 1 makes you vulnerable to thinking and feeling like the chickens around you do. Allowing your perspective to be stalled by your pack pulls you away from experiencing your personal true sense of clarity, confidence, and the conviction to take action on what has meaning for you.

It also pulls you away from experiencing a conscious, engaged way of living and working, and a connection to a sense of purpose.

The quote by Rumi at the beginning of this chapter—"Yesterday I was clever, so I wanted to change the world. Today I am wise, so I am changing myself"—offers caution for skipping over the Observation step. Skipping this step leaves you vulnerable for clarity on what we don't want or what we wish were happening faster. It also enables us to deny, ignore, or accept what is confusing, unknown, or depleting. All of those subtle nuances are forms of resistance. So when we feel confused, stuck, detached from a sense of purpose, or even burned out, we must allow ourselves to tune into the meaning we are making from what's happening around us. Focusing within enables our ability to surface ideas, recognize opportunities, or take actions that would have an actual chance of allowing a lasting sense of fulfillment for our work and our lives. Observing outside ourselves only fosters feeling confused, stuck, detached from a sense of purpose, and even burned out. As a result, the experiences and consequences that follow from either outlook gets bigger and more vivid in our life. The choice to focus within or externally is ours.

Burnout, just like a connection with purpose, is never a coincidence. It is a consequence. If you want to have a job you love instead of one that diminishes you on a soul level, practice awareness about what you are thinking, your urges for action, and feelings that surface within you. That way you won't keep creating what's keeping you exactly where you don't want to be—feeling confused, stuck, detached from a sense of purpose, or burned out.

Do you find it very hard to get in touch with your thoughts, urges, and feelings? If so, start with the distinction of where you are aligning your faith—toward the "hope" or the "fear" end of the Faith Spectrum.

Hope versus Fear

What you *do* and what you *express* will never give you more power than what you *believe*. So let's dive deep into faith, hope, fear, conviction, and courage. When we explore why they matter, we begin to recognize when we might be vulnerable to being less than engaged for our work. Don't worry, I will not take you on a guided meditation to your best or worst religious experiences. But I do want to discuss faith, because it's a relevant muscle you will want to develop further for experiencing work you love.

Merriam-Webster's definitions of *hope* are "to cherish a desire with anticipation; to desire with expectation of obtainment; to expect with confidence." Hope welcomes the possibility of virtuous outcomes.

When you are hopeless, you can't see the potential for good. Perhaps feeling hopeless is why you are reading this book. Is there something you feel you don't have that you see to be critical for your happiness or success? Perhaps your feelings of hopelessness aren't that you can't believe there is a possibility for good things in life, but that you just can't see how to discover or manifest them. Not being able to connect with hope doesn't mean hope is lost or doesn't exist. It's just about understanding where you have been putting your faith.

Merriam-Webster's non-religious definitions of faith are "a firm belief in something for which there is no proof; complete trust; something that is believed especially with strong conviction." I think of faith as having a spectrum attached to it. You will notice that one end of the spectrum below is negative and the other end is positive.

Faith Spectrum

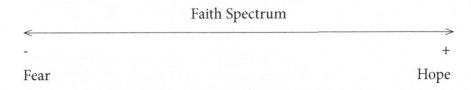

Your beliefs are what you trust, have confidence in, and hold as truth. In essence it's about what you have faith in, "good" or "bad." Faith toward the positive end of the spectrum is aligning with hope—the "good" you believe *could* happen. Faith toward the negative end of the spectrum is aligning with fear—the "bad" you believe *could* happen. Remember,

> Faith toward the positive end of the spectrum is aligning with hope—the "good" you believe *could* happen. Faith toward the negative end of the spectrum is aligning with fear—the "bad" you believe *could* happen.

"stress" is corporate jargon for "fear." So, whether positive or negative, when we put trust in what we believe, we are happier than a pig in s*#! And that is usually what we get when we believe from a place of fear. So in essence, "practicing faith" is merely practicing what you believe. There is a common saying "hope is not a plan." Hope may not be a plan, but it is a necessary mindset for soul-fulfilling visions, plans, actions, and results to be born. If you want to enjoy true success, it makes sense to get clear about your hope-based beliefs—what you actually want versus what you don't want. Agreed? Hope-based beliefs are what enable a true and sustainable sense of happiness more easily.

If you are unsure about the thoughts, urges, and feelings you are experiencing, try asking yourself, "Am I holding a perspective that is more aligned with hope or with fear?" When you answer this question, you will know that you do have faith and if you have faith toward fear, it's not a bad thing. It just provides the opportunity to get clear on what you believe is possible. In essence, this is what is known as the *Law of Polarity*. This law reflects that everything that exists has its opposite. The back of the hand has the front of the hand. The glass can be half full or half empty. Again, it is all about your mindset, which is simply your attitude. Are you choosing clarity for fear (e.g., overwhelm, overextension, disengagement, ineffectiveness, burnout), or for hope (e.g., peace, energy, civility, confidence, engagement)? Observe where your focus is.

I believe everything in the universe is designed for our growth and the unfolding of our consciousness—but not necessarily for our pleasure. Fear is a belief that the energy of the universe is out to do us harm. Fear constantly questions the wisdom of the universe's energy. It's questioning its intention or ability to bring benefit into our lives. Ask yourself, "How can this experience that seems negative actually be an opportunity for my growth?"

When you are in a situation that seems negative or harmful, Observe whether you can invite in benefits that could come from the situation and let go of the possibility that you will be led to anything bad. *Bad*, here, means *not* for your growth and the advancement of your consciousness. Try saying to

> Ask yourself, "How can this experience that seems negative actually be an opportunity for my growth?"

yourself or aloud to others, "I can't wait to see the benefits that come out of this situation." Saying this has nothing to do with ignoring the reality of a threatening situation. It merely adds room for hope—for a belief that something good, just as much as something bad, *could* come from the experience.

Just because events don't unfold the way we think they should does not mean the way they are unfolding will lead us to a different goal or result than we decided or intended for our lives. Deciding *what* we want for our lives is much more important than figuring out the details of *how* it should unfold.

Unattended fear keeps us stuck and clouds our ability to know ourselves or what we want. Attended fear can serve the purpose of building our energy so as to catapult us to a new level of love for and fulfillment from our work and life. It provides a velocity for knowing what we don't want, which we can transform into information about what we do want by just asking ourselves to imagine an opposite scenario. Not doing the work to create an opposite scenario from knowing what we don't want keeps us siding with fear. That only gives way to more fear and makes us vulnerable to prolonged feelings of being confused, overwhelmed, detached from a sense of purpose, or burnout.

When we use fear as information to be transformed into what we do want, we begin to align ourselves with what fulfills us. We also enable ourselves to recognize opportunities that can offer us the experiences we would welcome. Observing whether you are aligning closer to fear or hope (and seeing your choice to stay in that alignment or not) is key to healing from confusion, overwhelm, a lack of engagement, and burnout. If what we Observe is an alignment with fear, then we can embrace the gift of fear. Fear offers us *a signal* to notice and

Observe ourselves, face ourselves and our predicament, get clear about what we want to experience, and nurture ourself through the journey.

Observing—An Exercise

Here's an exercise involving your chakras. *Chakra* is a Sanskrit word that translates into English as "wheel." Chakras are energy fields in seven main areas in and around your body. These energy fields, when they are open and aligned with each other, efficiently receive and feed energy to our body. Therefore, they affect our emotional and physical wellness. I am not a chakra expert, nor am I a certified practitioner of anything that involves the use of the chakras for physical healing. I have, however, used the chakras as a way to gain some insight into what might trigger or keep me feeling upset or stuck.

In my research on chakras, I find that each source of information categorizes the expression of the chakras and the body parts they govern a bit differently. Some meditation classes teach that the chakras have positive (or, as I say, *hope-centric*) and negative (or, as I say, *fear-centric*) charges. I find this very inspiring for using the chakras in my work.

Below I offer you how I make sense and use of the chakras by their location, color representation, hope-centric and fear-centric charges, and my recommended actions for how we might nurture ourselves through blocked chakra experiences.

Chakra, location and color	fear and ego in charge	hope and soul in charge
Root—the base of the spine. red, brown, black, or grey	fear-focused, distrust in life, abandonment or disconnection, boredom, stuck, confusion, ungrounded, uncertain, hunger, longing for something, ashamed of your family or roots, lack of soul care	health, trust, boundaries, security, relaxed, caring for the basic needs of the self and/or family

*If your thinking or urges or feelings identify more with fear or the ego, try any of the following remedies related to **stability and survival** that would enable you to feel nurtured.*	*self-care for hygiene, health, safety and/or survival; forgiveness of self; acceptance of self and others; connection with those you love; getting your financial or personal affairs in order; cleaning, organizing and/or decorating your home, garden or landscape; nutrition and healthy meals; calming and restorative exercises*	
Chakra, location and color	**fear and ego in charge**	**hope and soul in charge**
Sacral—lower abdomen below the navel. orange	lust, vanity, greed, focus on or desire for material things, creatively blocked, judgmental, indifferent or apathetic, compulsive, overindulgent, guilt, joyless, vulnerable, doubtful	creativity, connection with others, playful, beautifying the self, spiritual awareness, charitable to others, learning
*If your thinking or urges or feelings identify more with fear or the ego, try any of the following remedies related to **creativity and pleasure** that would enable you to feel nurtured.*	*self-discovery; charitable acts, generosity and/or giving to others; creating more balance in your life; fun or pleasure; art and crafts or creativity; Observation of thoughts, urges and/or feelings; small acts that move you out of your comfort zone; self-help to build self-esteem; making love with a committed partner; movement-focused (i.e., Tai-chi, dance, yoga) or lower body exercises*	

Chakra, location and color	fear and ego in charge	hope and soul in charge
Solar plexus—stomach above the navel. yellow	low or no energy, childish, victimized, selfish or abusive to the self, blameful, manipulative, controlling, ashamed of self, unworthy	confident, energetic, openness to change or exploration, action and movement, faces challenges, powerful, disciplined, reliable, empathetic, grateful
If your thinking, urges and/or feelings identify more with fear or the ego, try any of the following remedies related to taking action or initiating a change that would enable you to feel nurtured.	*self-improvement;* *getting into action;* *acts of courage;* *practicing gratitude;* *seeking to understand self and others;* *noticing and following gut instincts;* *professional help to build self-esteem, heal trauma or anger, or reduce stress;* *vigorous (i.e., running, strength training) activity or abdominal exercises*	
Chakra, location and color	**fear and ego in charge**	**hope and soul in charge**
Heart—the center of the chest. green or pink	anger, divisive and rejecting of others, intolerant or critical of others, shaming, bullying, abusive and/or punishing to others, conditional, unloving to self or others, demanding, codependent, jealous, vengeful, no regard for the boundaries of self or others, enabler of others' destructive behavior, selfish or entitled	loving, kind, social, inclusive, respectful of others as well as the self, collaborative, passionate for life, grateful, altruistic, vibrant and healthy

If your thinking, urges and/or feelings identify more with fear or the ego, try any of the following remedies related to **love or balance** that would enable you to feel nurtured.	love of self and others; loving acts (i.e., random acts of kindness or generosity, practicing patience); noticing and following what your heart says; expression of feelings or gratitude; professional help for deep self-discovery, finding and exercising boundaries, forgiveness and relationship work, or healing from grief or loss; focusing on the breath (i.e., pranayama, breathwork); balance-focused fitness (i.e., yoga, reiki), aerobic, endurance, or chest exercises	
Chakra, location and color	**fear and ego in charge**	**hope and soul in charge**
Throat—throat. blue	gluttony, withholding your voice or opinion, sending mixed or deceptive messages, secretive, difficulty describing feelings, excessive talking, interrupts, gossipy, verbal abuse, lies, poor sense of ethics, poor sense of rhythm or tone-deaf	authentic; truthful; communicative; listens and hears what is said, implied and meant; clear messaging; expresses feelings or emotions without harming others
If your thinking, urges and/or feelings identify more with fear or the ego, try any of the following remedies related to **truth and self-expression** that would enable you to feel nurtured.	self-expression; learning and/or teaching; seeking information, advice or guidance; allowing yourself to say what needs to be said or speak your truth; singing and performing; developing communication skills (i.e., non-violent communication); practicing silence; guided meditation; activities focused on hearing and sound (i.e., sound therapy, music lessons, music that nurtures your soul); neck and shoulder massage	

Chakra, location and color	fear and ego in charge	hope and soul in charge
Third eye—forehead between your eyebrows. indigo	making excuses or procrastinating, attracted to frightening or horrific content (graphic images of violence, war, death), dismissive of intuitive notions, dreams or nightmares, experiences headaches or vision problems, poor memory, lack of concentration, lack of imagination, denial, delusion and confusion	intuitive, discerning, logical, perceptive, imaginative, good memory, vivid memorization of dreams, self-aware, self-reflective, able to manage and recover from stress in a healthy way, able to conceptualize and visualize for breakthrough results, rational and spiritual balance, recognizes patterns others may not see.
If your thinking, urges and/or feelings identify more with fear or the ego, try any of the following remedies related to a sense of higher self-knowing or intuitive trust that would enable you to feel nurtured.	*holistic self-discovery of mind, body, and soul; purpose-driven living and working; seeking professional and personal relationships that are supportive, mutually satisfying, and promoting of growth; visualization or future-focused activities; meditation; noticing and following intuition; creating or experiencing visual art (art therapy)*	

Chakra, location and color	fear and ego in charge	hope and soul in charge
Crown—the very top to slightly above your head. violet, white, or gold	detached from soul, isolated, egocentric, addiction, mental, emotional and personality disorders	soul-centric, hope-focused, peaceful, trusting of life, spiritual, conscious and enlightened, wise, connected and unified with others and all things
*If your thinking, urges and/or feelings identify more with fear or the ego, try any of the following remedies related to **unity, spiritual connection, growth and peace** that would enable you to feel nurtured.*	*spiritual connection;* *selfless and compassionate action (without regard for personal gain or return);* *acts of unity, oneness, and peace;* *spiritual practice (i.e., prayer);* *spiritual retreats or education;* *exercises that calm the mind*	

Note: The fear-centric expressions of blocked chakras are not meant to be represented as "bad". Instead, they can merely be seen as signals to take action by practicing the OPEN Method. The remedies are suggested strategies for nurturing yourself during times of closed or blocked chakra experiences.

Denying the experience of a fear-centric thought, urge, or feeling and/or not nurturing yourself through it is what creates stuck energy in the body as well as in all aspects of life, including work.

When using the chakras as a tool, I identify where in my body I Observe the energy of my thought, urge, and/or feeling. That gives me insight into the essence of my issue. I do that by asking myself *Where in my body do I sense my thought, urge, and/or feeling?*

Consider the work of Louise Hay, the iconic self-help pioneer, founder of Hay House Publishing, and author of the breakthrough book, *You Can Heal Your Life*. There, she talks about the mind-body connection. Louise explains that what we believe about ourselves is often a catalyst of our emotional and physical state. In its simplest essence, the mind-body connection means that how we think and feel—whether consciously or subconsciously—strongly influences our wellness. For example, fear-based thoughts, urges and/or feelings that go unattended manifest in the body as illness or other conditions. We can improve our health and the quality of our lives when we change our thinking by addressing our fear-based thoughts, urges, and/or feelings. The mind-body connection is also known as Somatic Psychotherapy, which is the study of our internal state on our body and our wellness. I infer that you can get deeper insight into what and why things are being triggered based on where unexpressed thoughts, urges, or feelings might be expressing their energy in your body. The chakras affected might provide ideas for how to nurture yourself through challenges and restore capacity for engagement.

Here is a simple view of the body areas governed by each chakra:

- **root chakra**—spine, bones, blood cells, and colon

- **sacral chakra**—pelvis, legs, reproductive organs, and kidneys

- **solar plexus chakra**—abdominals, lower back, digestive organs, liver, and muscles, the ego

- **heart chakra**—heart, chest, mid-back, breasts, arms, blood flow

- **throat chakra**—throat, upper back, shoulders, jaw, neck, ears

- **third eye chakra**—forehead, brow, left brain or analytical mind, consciousness

- **crown chakra**—right brain or creative mind, subconscious mind, the soul and ego working together

When a problem arises, I ask the question: *Where in my body do I sense my thought, urge, and/or feeling?* Not only will the answer identify

where the problem is settling but it can also give me insight into remedial activities that can help me feel nurtured to face and resolve problems productively.

Next I ask, *What color is my thought, urge, or feeling?*

Each chakra relates to one or more colors. The color might point
to a chakra that holds the answer for why I am experiencing this challenge, as well as to remedial activity that could help me to feel nurtured
to face and resolve problems productively. Consider the chakra colors:

- red, brown, black, or grey—root chakra
- orange—sacral chakra
- yellow—solar plexus chakra
- green or pink—heart chakra
- blue—throat chakra
- indigo—third eye chakra
- violet, white, or gold—crown chakra

Next I ask, *What might this energy's location in my body and the color I
sense from it be trying to tell me?*

- If the energy is sensed as red, brown, black, or grey or it's in
  the root chakra, is there something you need to stick with, get
  grounded about, consider how it affects your family, values, or
  core beliefs?

- If the energy is sensed as the color orange or it's in the sacral
  chakra, is there something that needs to be creatively solved or
  an allowance made for fun or pleasure to be experienced?

- If the energy is sensed as the color yellow or it's in the solar
  plexus chakra, is there an action you need to take?

- If the energy is sensed as the color green or pink or it's in the heart
  chakra, is there something that needs to be loved or nurtured?

- If the energy is sensed as the color blue or it's in the throat chakra, is there something that needs to be expressed or communicated?

- If the energy is sensed as the color indigo or it's in the third eye chakra, is there something that needs to be seen in a new way?

- If the energy is sensed as violet, white, or gold or it's in the crown chakra, how is what you are experiencing providing an opportunity for your growth?

Often this layered exercise can reveal either the essence of your problem or what to do to take care of yourself while experiencing a challenging time. For example, if there is a pain or weakness in your legs, and the color you imagine the pain to be is yellow, try asking yourself a question related to the sacral (legs) and solar plexus chakras (yellow). For example, is there an unfulfilled desire for fun (the legs—chakra of fun, pleasure, and creativity) creating blocked energy because of lack of action (yellow—chakra related to action)?

When you are feeling blocked in any of the chakras, try including one of the recommended actions from the chakra below it to power up on hope-centric energy. In our example above, for instance, you might try remedies from the root chakra (one chakra below sacral chakra) to surface clarity for the block in the legs, which are governed by the sacral chakra.

Another example is if you feel an unusual energy in your throat chakra and it's orange, try one action recommendation from the heart chakra (the chakra below throat), as well as one from the orange, sacral chakra. What enables our ability to access hope-centric energy comes from lower chakras and travels upward toward the crown chakra. Unexpressed or unhealed fear-centric experiences manifest as energy that travels downward from higher chakras toward the root chakra. Simply put, hope-centric energy flows up and fear-centric energy flows down.

> Hope-centric energy flows up and fear-centric energy flows down.

Here is an example of a college student who applied this exercise to a challenge she was facing. The student, let's refer to her as June, was feeling fed up with college and felt urges to quit. June frequently cried over her situation and was beginning to experience discomfort in her body. In applying this exercise, she identified that she frequently felt the sensation of an urge to quit in her chest (the heart chakra) and that the color was red.

June considered the fear-centric and hope-centric expressions of the heart chakra (she felt a stuck energy; *what* was stuck?) and the root chakra (the color of the blocked energy was red; *why* is it stuck?). She resonated with a lack of passion for her major and with a lack of love and care for herself as to what could be blocking clarity for what to do about college. The clue for being stuck came from the color she sensed—red means root chakra. June deliberated over whether she was holding onto societal expectations to graduate high school, go on to college, and get a job doing something where she could make a reasonable salary, or whether she was holding on to perceived family expectations of who she was supposed to be. To honor her true self and feel passion for her major, she wondered whether she needed to find her own way even if it meant going against what she thought society or her family might have expected of her or wanted for her. Could her sense of stability or some structure for her life be threatened in some way if she pursued something she loved and could be passionate about?

Through such questions, and nurturing herself through the remedial actions offered by both chakras (heart and root chakras), it came to her that she would change her major from nursing to agriculture. So instead of healing people (her initial major was nursing), she decided healing the Earth would be a better alignment with her soul. With that decision, she became confident to pivot to a path of purpose and allow her family and friends to have their own opinions about her choice without them affecting how she viewed herself and her life possibilities. June then approached college with a more soul-fulfilling (and therefore ego-nurturing) approach.

Sometimes with this exercise, insight into how to use your thinking, urges, and/or feelings as signals to move forward with purpose is immediate. Sometimes, nurturing actions from both chakras might be helpful in order to naturally surface purposeful action over time. Whether insights surface for you immediately or not, what matters most is to give yourself the gift of time to allow answers to surface. Healing is rarely an on-demand exercise.

> Human beings manifest what they have faith in.

Human beings manifest what they have faith in. Observe yourself and recognize that you do have a choice between a hope-centric (soul-nurturing) or fear-centric (ego-nurturing) approach to work. Observing yourself might be an act of courage for you. It's time to get courageous, face your Observed fear and ask yourself to imagine an opposite (a hope-focused) perspective. No longer settle for clarity only on what you don't want.

I often suggest to my clients who struggle with facing their Observed fear to find an image of the Fearless Girl statue facing the Charging Bull statue in NYC and set that image on their smart phone or computer as their screen saver. It is a reminder to be fearless and face what evokes fear for you. If Observation is an act of courage for you, here are some of the things you can do to soothe yourself through your moment of Observation. Do one:

- hold your own hands
- make a fist out of your hand, place it on your heart and gently tap the center of your chest several times
- crisscross your arms to rest a hand on each of your shoulders
- rub your hands on your thighs or knees
- give yourself a hug and rub your back if possible

In other words, touch yourself the way you would offer comfort to another who is crying or upset. Be your own friend by giving yourself a gesture of love and support.

The first step of facing and dealing with anything is to acknowledge it and notice how it is affecting you. Give yourself the opportunity to try an alternative to Observing anything outside yourself. Let go of analyzing how another person or a situation should be affecting you. Let go of how you believe you should be reacting or responding. Instead, notice and Observe what actually is. See your truth—mind, body, and soul.

> The first step of facing and dealing with anything is to acknowledge it and notice how it is affecting you.

CHAPTER 7

STEP 2—PAUSE FOR THE P IN OPEN

Between stimulus and response there is a space. In that space is our power to choose our response. In our response lies our growth and our freedom.

Stephen R. Covey

Give Yourself a Break—Decide When You Will Take Action

Pause is Step 2. This step has nothing to do with *doing* anything. In this step, we ask the question, *"How long do I need to just be with my thoughts, urges, and feelings?"*

For me, the answer varies depending on the situation and my ability to digest it. No matter what, the Pause is always temporary.

To Pause is to temporarily stop and just be with your observed thoughts, urges, and feelings without doing anything about them. Don't judge, reject, or try to avoid them. Just be with them.

Pausing is usually not necessary when we are experiencing hope-filled thoughts, urges, and feelings because we are typically already open and able to respond in a productive manner. Pausing is usually a short break that can last a few minutes or hours but it may

be longer when we are experiencing
intensely stressful (fear-filled) thoughts,
urges, and feelings. This step is important
because when we experience fear-filled
thoughts, urges, and feelings, we initially
might experience a block from being able
to recognize what could be productive
and nurturing. Often, just giving yourself time is enough to allow your soul to
return to the driver's seat. How much time to Pause is unique for each
person and each situation, there is no rule to follow.

> Pause and just be with
> your observed thoughts,
> urges, and feelings
> without doing anything.
> Don't judge, reject, or try
> to avoid them. Just be
> with them.

To Pause is also to make a preliminary decision about how long
feels right to just be with yourself. For me, I usually want just a few
minutes. Sometimes I want longer and either way I give that time to
myself. That means, I do not worry about doing anything other than
being with what I think, what I have an urge to do or say, and what I
feel. I also postpone asking myself any questions about how to solve,
fix, or change my thinking, urges, and/or feelings.

When no answer comes about when to move forward, simply
decide when you will ask yourself the question again. Again, just ask
yourself, *How long would feel right to think my thoughts, and feel my
urges and feelings without taking any action on them?*

Denying, ignoring, or containing our soul-centric thoughts, urges,
and feelings doesn't feel good, so it's not shocking that doing that with
our egocentric ones won't work either. How long thoughts, urges and
emotions might last depend on how meaningful something is to us,
how detrimental it is, plus what we do about it.[13]

No one likes to be denied, ignored, stifled, or told they are wrong
for their thoughts, urges, or feelings. Upsets of any kind are often better
responded to after taking a moment to just be still without judgment or
guilt. Giving yourself a Pause is like sitting with a friend, listening to them,
holding their hand, or giving them a hug when they are upset. During

> During Pause, you are both the friend in need and the friend who is offering support, comfort, and love.

Pause, you are both the friend in need and the friend who is offering support, comfort, and love. But how do you do that when the trigger of your upset is right there in front of you—especially at your job?

When you observe thoughts, urges, or feelings that are draining, this step asks you to remove yourself momentarily and immediately from the situation or people upsetting you. This will give you some space and room to breathe. Simply say, "I need a moment of time to digest that. Would you be willing to let me get back to you when I feel ready to move forward?"

If that request is not honored, you can simply listen and reiterate that you don't feel ready to offer anything that would be productive and again state your desire to postpone further discussion until you feel ready to respond productively. If that should fail, you always have the option to simply say, "Please excuse me." Or say nothing at all and just walk away without anger, judgment, or guilt. Pausing (which may include just walking away) is an active step that ushers in energy that will enable productive interactions and solutions to surface.

Pause Exercise—A Mini-Practice in Action

Pause is my favorite part of the OPEN Method and it's what enabled me to quit smoking for good. Here's my cigarette story, which was the birth of the OPEN Method and *Pause Mini-Practices*. I call this particular mini-practice the *Purge the Urge* mini-practice.

When I was in my twenties, I was what I would call a casual, social smoker. That meant I typically smoked in the evening after work, when I was on vacation, or when I was out having fun with friends. I never went through more than one pack a week. Nonetheless, I wanted to quit. I tried a variety of techniques to quit and still I found it challenging to stop once and for all. At first I just went cold turkey. That lasted until the next time I saw my friends and we went out for drinks. I tried hypnosis, which was great for a few months, but then I was right back into my usual social smoking routine. Then my employer offered *Smokenders* support so I tried that approach. It too lasted for a few months but over time I slowly went back to smoking. Shortly after my thirtieth birthday, I came down with bronchitis. That was so awful I decided I was going to attempt quitting again.

I knew willpower alone wouldn't last long so I was looking for a new support program. But then something happened that had never happened before. One day, while at work, I had an urge to have a cigarette. I wasn't sure what to do. Thankfully, I didn't have any cigarettes on me. Nor did I want to ask anyone I worked with for a cigarette since I hid that little secret from the people at my corporate job. At that time of my life, I had learned enough about meditation to know I sucked at it and hated it, but feeling no options to turn to, I simply closed my office door, turned off the lights, sat in my office chair, and closed my eyes for my own version of meditation.

I sat, eyes closed, with my pumps on the floor, my back straight, and pressed against the chair's ergonomic lumbar support. My tailored suit skirt held my knees together and I placed my hands in my lap. My elbows enjoyed support from the arm rests of my chair. Focusing on my breath stressed me out and often put me into hyperventilation. Trying to empty my thoughts seemed harder than trying to figure out brain surgery. So instead, I allowed my mind to be directed by a question that popped into my brain. The question was *"What does it feel like to want?"*

With that question, I began to observe how "wanting" felt for me. I quickly noticed my back was slightly arching, my chest felt anxious, and my breathing was shallow and quick. My hands felt as though they could start twitching at any moment, even though they were still. My jaw was tight and tingly, my legs wanted to stretch and move, and I wanted to rotate my ankles until I heard snapping, cracking, popping noises. Yet I just sat there.

I thought to myself, *Wow, you're doing it! You are experiencing what it feels like to want!*

I was amazed at my ability to experience this without taking action since action is my automatic mode. I was so dazzled by this experience, I started asking myself, *What else happens when you experience "want"?* I began making plans to leave work precisely at 5:00 p.m. to have a cigarette at home on my back deck, which faces the woods. Alone, secluded, and indulging in a smoke—*yum!* I also thought about who I could possibly bum a cigarette from at work without feeling too exposed. I was beyond impressed with how my mind could visualize, strategize, plan, and savor the benefits while weighing the risks of each option.

Look at you go! I said to myself. I kept going, letting my mind and body crank out ideas and demands for attention. I then noticed it wasn't really about a cigarette anymore, it was just about experiencing "want." Suddenly, it wasn't about "want," it was then about gratitude. Gratitude for an office with a door I could shut and disappear into for a few quiet moments. I noticed each second I felt "want," but I also felt gratitude in having the power to not react to that urge.

And then I observed something else I never expected to experience.

Suddenly I no longer wanted a cigarette nor did I feel the need to continue this adventure into "Gina's World of Want." Instead I felt calm, at peace, grateful, relaxed, and in touch with a side of myself I didn't know existed. A resourceful, powerful, soul-nurturing side that assured me I would always be okay as long as I was taking care of myself. When I opened my eyes I was shocked to see that about twenty minutes had gone by when it felt like less than ten minutes. I went on with my day and was fine. I never did have that cigarette when I got home.

The urge for a cigarette came up again a few days later and I repeated the exercise. That time the urge for "want" passed in less than twenty minutes. This happened to me only about two or three more times. Just enough for me to notice that every time it did come up, my experience to respond to my urge for a cigarette was shorter and shorter until it never came up again.

I didn't know what I was doing at the time, but without realizing it, I was learning what Carl Jung taught us about how what we resist *persists* (and even grows in size) and what Dr. David Hawkins wrote about years later in *Letting Go: The Pathway of Surrender.* Surrendering is key to moving forward whenever you are faced with a challenge. I learned it wasn't about resisting an urge for a smoke, but surrendering to the experience of an urge—to the experience of "want." I unwittingly practiced the Pause step by allowing myself to just be with my thoughts, urges, and feelings related to smoking without doing anything about them. The persistent ability to just be with my thoughts, urges, and feelings whenever the urge for a cigarette came up not only got me past the habit of smoking, it also developed a process that worked for me to get through other draining situations in my life.

> By observing and pausing, I learned it wasn't about resisting an urge for a smoke, but surrendering to the experience of an urge—to the experience of "want."

Don't be afraid to surrender to an experience of your thoughts, urges, or feelings. Often, we are so focused on what triggers us or the "bad" that could come from our thought, urge, or feeling that we overlook the gift of the space between stimulus and response.

More Pause Mini-Practices—Try Them!

Pause Mini-Practices require no work at all. They simply allow you to experience your thoughts, urges, and feelings in order to surface *response* versus *reaction* for others and ideas for self-care for yourself. In this step, you temporarily take yourself off the hook for strategies, solutions, and actions. You don't need to torture yourself with self-judgment or guilt in order to surface a beautiful and nurturing alternative.

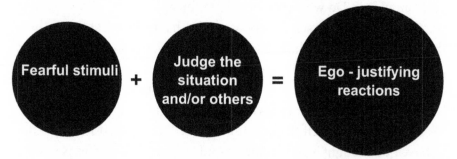

The Path to Burnout Offers *React* Experiences

Fearful stimuli **+** Judge the situation and/or others **=** Ego - justifying reactions

The Path of Purpose Offers *Respond* Experiences

Fearful stimuli **+** Pause to be with your self observations **=** Soul - validating responses

Despite this step requiring nothing of you, sometimes it helps to have a few things *to do* to remind yourself you are in the Pause phase. These mini-practices can help you calm down your ego and surface your soul. You'll know it's happening because a feeling of calm peace will come over you. Pick one of these mini-practices to try next time you are faced with uncomfortable thoughts, urges, or feelings.

Option A—The Purge-the-Urge Mini-Practice

If you are faced with an uncomfortable thought, urge, or feeling, try my *Purge-the-Urge Mini Practice*. I did it when I wanted to move past an urge for a cigarette at work:

First: Sit comfortably and quietly for a few moments with eyes closed, feet on the floor, back straight, and hands on your thighs. Your arms could also be crisscrossed over your chest with your hands on your shoulders. Do whatever feels right for you.

Second: Ask yourself the question, "What does it feel like to have this thought, urge, feeling?" Observe what your body wants to do when faced with this question. Observe the ideas, thoughts, or images created by your mind when faced with this question. Observe the feelings that surface when faced with this question.

Third: Ask yourself the question again: "What else does it feel like to have this thought, urge, feeling?" Did any new observations surface when faced with this question a second time?

Fourth: Ask your ego the question a third time: "Is there anything more you, my ego, want to say about this thought, urge, feeling?" Do any new observations surface when you confront your ego directly with this question a third time?

Finally: Stay with yourself until you notice that your ego has finished expressing itself and a sense of peace, calm, or gratitude washes over you. That is your soul surfacing.

A friend of mine shared with me that my "Purge the Urge" mini-practice helped her move past her pattern of overindulging in a nightly ritual of eating chocolate ice cream during the COVID 19 pandemic.

Option B—The Going-Within Mini-Practice

Simply direct your attention within for a few minutes. You can do this by sitting in a quiet spot, closing your eyes, and focusing your thoughts and observations. This might look like an intentional thought such as a meditation mantra or prayer. It could also be an intentional observation of your breath or heartbeat for a few minutes.

Option C—The What-About-Water? Mini-Practice

Take a relaxing bath or shower. Some of my most creative ideas and solutions have come to me in the shower. If it's raining outside, an alternative to the shower is just sitting with your eyes closed and listening to the rain. There are also great recordings of the sound of rain and of ocean waves available from your favorite place to access music. I often like to fall asleep to those tracks.

Option D—The Earth-Under-My-Feet Mini-Practice

Go outside, take off your shoes and socks, and walk on the grass— soaking in the electrons from the earth offers us a great exposure to antioxidants. This is called the practice of grounding, or earthing. I read an article by Carrie Dennett in *The Washington Post*, explaining that walking barefoot on the earth can lower stress as well as have other positive physiological effects.[14] I used to love having an evening glass of wine outside after a full day at work. Now I'm more inclined to skip the wine—and my shoes—and take in a moment to soak up some Earth energy while drinking water.

Option E—The Mind, Body, Soul Moment Mini-Practice

Try any type of meditation, visualization, stretching, or prayer. With meditation and visualization, there are so many guided practice options out there to learn about and try. It's easy to do a Google search on meditation to find one that speaks to you or you can simply spend a moment with any of the many apps (e.g., Calm or Headspace) that offer different techniques for Pausing. You don't need to invest twenty to thirty minutes to connect with your mind, body, or soul. You only need to be aware that you are taking a moment to do so.

To Pause your mind, focus intensely on one thing for a few seconds to two minutes. With your body, it can be as simple as standing up, stretching, and taking a moment of silence before you sit down and get back to work. With your soul, it can be internally reciting your favorite prayer, affirmation, poem, quote, or saying to yourself. You can also try what I call a *soul chat*.

Option F—The Soul Chat Mini-Practice

A *soul chat* is when I ask my soul to speak to another person's soul. I ask my soul to tell the other person's soul about a boundary that I have and want respected between us. Sometimes it's about a wish I have for them or for the both of us. No matter which, I always ask our souls to *cocoon* together in peace, light, and love.

In summary, feeling calm and peaceful while you are just being with yourself (your thoughts, urges, and feelings) is the goal of the Pause step. Social media sites are definitely to be avoided during the Pause step since they stimulate the ego and distract your attention away from surfacing your soul side.

The step known as Pause in the OPEN Method is the opportunity to be with what you observed in Step 1—Observe and to experience the gift of the space between stimulus and response. You do this so that clarity about what would be nurturing to your soul can emerge. The power of Step 2 should never be overlooked.

CHAPTER 8

STEP 3—ENGAGE FOR THE E IN OPEN

When you consistently choose the things that bring about a state of expansion in you, it dramatically increases your experience of happiness and well-being.

Marci Shimoff

Engage—Figure It Out

In Step 1, I suggested you ask yourself an initial simple question whenever you are confronted with a problem or challenge. That question is *"Am I okay?"*

When your answer is *"No,"* the Pause in Step 2 is next. Just be with your initial reactive thoughts, urges, and feelings without the added burden of worrying or figuring anything out about how to address the situation, yourself, or others. Pausing matters because you never want to create solutions from the fear side (ego-driven) of the Faith Spectrum. In pausing, you decide how much time feels right to just experience your thoughts, urges, and feelings. This lasts until you have naturally returned to a state that is aligned with the hope side (soul-driven) of the Faith Spectrum. At that point you can transition into a state of readiness to restore depleted soul energy.

To Engage is to figure out what you will do to take care of yourself and restore your soul to the driver's seat. When the soul is back in the driver's seat, you feel equipped to face the situation you are dealing with. In identifying solutions that are soul-nurturing, you distract your focus from blame, fault-finding, judgment, and/or guilt about your depleting experience. With your focus turned toward balancing your soul and ego, you destine yourself to experience a sense of clarity and reestablish your connection with a sense of purpose. Wouldn't that be better than to indulge blame, fault-finding, judgment, or guilt, which would destine you to more of what depletes you?

Once you are ready to move from Pause to Engage, ask yourself two questions:

1. "What can I give to myself that would feel soul-nurturing during this time of stress (fear)?" The easiest thing to do would be to check out your list of "Twenty-Five Things." Another option is to imagine that it's your best friend or child telling you they were feeling the way you are feeling. What would you say to them or do for them? You can say that to yourself and give that to yourself too! (I hope you didn't say, "Suck it up!").

2. "What would I appreciate from others to help me nurture my soul?" Advocating for what you value puts power in your corner. Taking care of yourself is essential. Whether or not you get what you would value from others isn't what matters most—it's additional. Of course, having others do what you want is nice but it's not what will restore you on a soul level. The act of advocating for yourself and asking for what you want is what will restore your soul. The receiving is optional.

This step has nothing to do with figuring out what will enable you to perform feats of emotional strength that might include a Mr. or Ms. Universe ability to kiss ass, avoid making waves (even though you are really disgusted by another's behavior), or solve any problems. Step three also has nothing to do with developing a fine talent for looking out for number one at the expense of others, while making it look like you care about others or the initiatives of the company you work for. If you are all about yourself at work, trust me, everyone knows it—you are fooling no one.

The goal of the Engage step is to figure out what you will do to nurture yourself so that the soul can restore, productive ideas can surface, and responsive actions are possible. The productive ideas may include clarity about what you will request of others as a means to make a meaningful difference for others, which enables the same for yourself in return. Although the main purpose of this step is figuring out how to care for yourself, sometimes ideas will pop up about what to do about your challenge.

> Your job in the Engage phase is simply about figuring out how to take care of yourself on a soul-fulfilling level.

Remember, your job in this phase is primarily to figure out what would feel nurturing to yourself; it is *not* to think up productive responses to your challenges. It is also not about converting fear to hope. It's simply about figuring out how to take care of yourself on a soul-fulfilling level. If ideas surface organically about how to address the challenge that depleted you, it's okay to welcome and consider them while you figure out care that's soul-nurturing. If ideas do surface quickly, postpone taking action on them if you can until you have given yourself some soul-nurturing care. If time is of the essence, then figure out what would feel nurturing to yourself *while* you address your challenge. And if ideas don't pop up, that is fine too.

When we are in a state of fear, we can still move forward with soul-nurturing acts from a place of *courage. Courage* is defined as "acting with a degree of fear" (*fear* as in having clarity about the bad things that *could* happen). Courage does not allow fear or confusion over what to do to nurture yourself to overcome a choice to make room for a hopeful outlook. Acknowledging your fear or lack of clarity and facing it can be as simple as asking yourself, "What would be an opposite state to the 'bad' I can clearly imagine happening?" Deciding to gain clarity about what you want versus what you don't want is doing the work to Engage in *open*ing a path of purpose. It doesn't matter whether you are more naturally inclined to know what you want or know what you don't want. Either disposition can lead you forward and keep you from feeling stuck. Feeling stuck, confused, detached from purpose, and burned out are the result of experiencing fear (stress) without doing anything to nurture and restore your soul. Sometimes we get to face fear with the conviction that comes from hope. Sometimes it comes from courage. Imagining opposite states to what you fear is more easily done when we know we are doing it as an act of soul-nurturing.

So, there is no need to pressure yourself into acting with courage or forcing a false sense of hope for your situation. You will be able to get there more naturally and authentically when you Engage in exploring and giving yourself what would feel nurturing.

The Value of Soul Care

There's more to self-care than taking care of your health and hygiene. I'm sure you agree that taking care of yourself (by eating well, exercising, drinking enough water, sleeping, as well as bathing, grooming, and dressing in ways that make you feel good) matters. What we may not realize is that managing our soul is also important for our well-being.

> Managing our soul is important for our well-being.

Well-being is different than *wellness*. *Wellness* is the external evidence of your internal *well-being*. *Well-being* is

1. knowing who you are, what you have to offer, and how to take care of yourself mind, body, and soul. This enables …

2. engagement. This enables …

3. a connection with a sense of purpose. This enables …

4. the capacity to joyfully receive and handle external and material rewards.

Well-being expands beyond promoting happiness. It's a holistic approach to unleash and maintain a soul-fulfilling sense of physical, financial, professional, emotional, and social well-being. When that is unleashed, it impacts all areas of your life, including how you feel about and perform at your job.

We must tap into a soul-fulfilling sense of well-being to enable ourselves to receive and handle material success. For example, I love it when clients tell me how much they want a job that allows them to have work-life balance. Meanwhile, they do things like never scheduling time off (justified by a million reasons why they can't), nor do they ever advocate for what would enable them to feel more balanced and supported at home or on the job. They are married to their stories about how balance is hard to achieve or impossible. In such cases, a flexible job schedule is never possible because they wouldn't know how to handle it if it hit them square between the eyes. Yet, their ego is convinced that balance is needed. *The fact that they are focused on reasons why balance isn't possible* usually means there's a belief that the ability to create balance exists outside themselves. Whenever we believe solutions are outside of ourselves, the ego is in the driver's seat. As a result, they struggle to experience balance because the ego is not open to being proven wrong.

Taking action by practicing the OPEN Method and advocating for balance (with courage if necessary) comes in handy for restoring the soul. Doing so enables material rewards such as an opportunity for a flexible work schedule that can be virtuously received. This does not happen the other way around.

Such a soul-fulfilling approach for balance demonstrates that you care about and are ready for your well-being. In order for employers or anyone else to be open to you, you must be open with yourself first. Practice *the OPEN Method to demonstrate you are ready!*

If you don't know what well-being looks like for you, no one else will see well-being in you either. What we do for our well-being demonstrates that we love ourself for who we are and what we can enable for others, and we value what is soul-fulfilling. Our willingness to explore who we are, what has meaning for us, and advocating for it so that we can be our best self for those we serve is walking the path of purpose. It's time to recognize that self-*care* includes *soul care* and is not selfish. It's a necessary step for healing from chronic overwhelm and the dimensions of burnout, restoring engagement, and securing a connection with a sense of purpose.

One thing I learned from Louise Hay's book, *How to Love Yourself, Cherishing the Incredible Miracle that You Are* is that the quickest way to recover from feeling trapped and burned out is to discover (or rediscover) who you are and love yourself for it. It's amazing how we change what we notice as an opportunity and how deeply we engage in our work and life when we shift how we view and care for ourselves—for our *soul*.

If you are feeling stuck, confused, detached from a sense of purpose, or burned out at work, you *can* get off this slippery slope and recover.

Create Your Personal Power Practice

Just as you would start a fitness routine to shed some weight, invest in the right sneakers to run a marathon, or attend regular appointments at a salon for grooming, a Personal Power Practice matters too. A Personal Power Practice is soul-nurturing care that helps you keep your well-being capacity in top shape. It includes several factors:

1. **an active decision** to participate in what can help strengthen your feeling of personal power,

2. **a regular practice** to seek always to grow your personal power experience,

3. **sharing** your Personal Power Practice experiences with others: what you are experiencing, learning about yourself, and how you are taking care of your mind, body, *and soul* versus sharing your fear-fueled thoughts and feelings on how others irritate you or should change. (BTW, how are those Purpose Partner discussions going?)

Why adopt a Personal Power Practice? Here are some things that are in it for you:

- an ability to think and act more calmly, clearly, and productively,
- personal control over your urges,
- an ability to know and address your feelings productively,
- a mindset that comes from a sense of personal power,
- an ability to discover and offer your talents more easily,
- higher performance more naturally; more *effort* may not be necessary
- improved capacity for civility and cooperation with others,
- more energy to face your day,
- an ability to bounce back from setbacks more easily,
- improved creativity,
- professional development,
- personal growth,
- clarity that you matter,
- confidence that you can make a meaningful difference for others,
- connection to a sense of purpose,
- conviction for your purpose.

In short you gain clarity, confidence, and conviction for your work and life. You can experience vigor versus exhaustion; civility and dedication versus cynicism; and a sense of accomplishment and personal power versus powerlessness.

No matter what your limiting self-beliefs might be, know that you are stuck there because you focused on external factors during times of stress.

You shift your focus from your stressors to your sense of personal power when you ask yourself the two questions of the Engage step:

Q1: "What can I give to myself that would feel soul-nurturing during this time of stress (fear)?"

Q2: "What would I appreciate from others to help me nurture my soul?"

You might be wondering how big the nurturing gesture should be. Let me answer that for you with a simple analogy.

When my kids were much smaller, one of their "biggest stressors" was the nightly dose of green vegetables that showed up on their plate. To them, it was a pile of sludge that acted as a barrier between them and their favorite desserts. No matter how good for them those vegetables were, nothing I was going to say would convince them to see the opportunity those vegetables brought them. I was just the big, bad, mean boss who subjected them to this nightly torture.

I knew that the way they saw those vegetables was tough for them and it was downright draining for everyone! What I taught them about eating their vegetables is the same thing I am going to teach you about how grand a gesture your nurturing actions must be to get yourself through tough times and restore your soul.

Think of the vegetables as the stressor you face, and dessert as something that you love, brings you joy, and restores you on a soul level.

- If my kids chose to eat none of the vegetables (no stress), there would not be any dessert. Nothing lost—nothing gained.

- If they chose to eat some of the vegetables (some stress), there would be some dessert. Some lost—some gained.

- If they chose to eat *all* of the vegetable (a lot of stress), they could have *as much dessert as they wanted*. A lot lost—all you could ever want *and then some* gained!

We can't always choose what we will face but we can always choose the degree to which we will Engage in soul-nurturing practices so we restore and build our fortitude to face our challenges. When we don't feel that we have reliable, ongoing access to what fills us up, we will feel like we are not in control of our ability to respond—we will react. The truth is everything we do either adds to or takes away from our sense of fulfillment. It's okay to experience things that take away from our sense of fulfillment. Often those experiences are what enable us to learn, grow, and relate in a more meaningful way to others. They evolve our consciousness. Too often, we allow ourselves to do things that drain us, yet we do nothing to restore our fulfillment supply. Again, it's okay to experience something that is draining. It's not okay to do nothing to restore what's been drained. That would be like expecting a car to drive without gas.

> It's okay to experience something that is draining. It's not okay to do nothing to restore what's been drained.

We must learn to recognize when our soul is low in fulfillment (i.e., out of gas) as evidenced by thoughts, urges, and feelings that are closer to the fear end of the Faith Spectrum. Being low in this way at our job feels like overwhelm, exhaustion, cynicism, powerlessness, downright burned out, or detached from purpose. When we feel such things, we must stop judging them as bad, and just take it as a clue that it's time to give ourselves what we need to fuel up. Fueling up is a way to amp up our connection with our personal power and sense of purpose. If you practiced tending to your fulfillment tank on a regular basis, how differently would you show up for others? It's not just about showing up differently. Sometimes, especially when we are going through stressful times, it's about showing up at all!

Let me share something with you to drive this point into your heart.

Remember the Gallup study I mentioned in chapter 1 that found that less than 40 percent of working Americans are engaged at their job? A mentor of mine, Beth LeFevre, once made the analogy of imagining what would happen if less than 40 percent of your heart were working right. You'd be dead—your soul has *left the building*! Could a zombie apocalypse be playing out in the workforce?

Would it make a difference in your life, especially when you are going through stressful times, to nurture yourself on a soul level? Can you wake up, restore, and heal? Of course you can! Identifying the kind of care that would restore and nurture your soul is the goal for the Engage step.

Nurturing the Ego, and ONLY the Ego

Learning how to nurture yourself on a soul level includes learning the difference between doing things that you enjoy *and* are sustainable for fulfillment versus things that feel good but could actually be keeping you down. When we strive to nurture our ego, we sometimes do things that actually may not be in our best interest, especially if we do those things to excess. Doing things that nurture our ego isn't always "bad," but it may not give us soul fulfillment we can benefit from. It's like eating a candy bar or drinking an energy drink versus having healthy meals or getting adequate sleep every night. Candy and energy drinks may be a treat or do the trick for the short term, but if you truly are feeling chronically depleted, there's a reason. Could it be that you are depleted on a soul level? Be sure to Engage in acts that fulfill your soul, not just your ego. Remember, the ego seeks to protect itself from ever looking bad and settles for what feels good in the moment, no matter how detrimental the longer-term effects might be.

When we nurture our ego, what we experience is often more like a temporary escape from something that is draining to us. Often it involves one of the seven deadly sins: vanity, greed, lust, envy, gluttony, wrath, sloth. We are left feeling neutral, numb, or negative.

Are any of these phrases familiar?

- "Meh, it was ok*ay*."
- "I don't know."
- "Not enough! I want more!"
- "Oy! I'll regret that in the morning."
- "Oh man, I hope Mom doesn't find out about this."
- "Why did I do that? How stupid of me!"

When we settle for nurturing merely the ego, we find ourselves choked by worry, and exhausted by the chase for material gain or fleeting amusement. As a result, we become stunted in our ability to connect with and mature our conscience. We struggle to feel a lasting sense of connection with our unique ability to make a difference and feel connected to a sense of purpose. In essence, we might settle for complaining or laughing often at others' expense, as the primary means of establishing connection with others.

Nurturing our ego often looks like finding a sense of security and justification from things or people outside ourselves whom we can garner attention from. Nothing feels simple, easy, sustainable, or secure. Again, ego seeks justification. So when you nurture your ego you might be doing one or more of these:

- *Avoiding* by lying, denying, or being shy—anything to get away from something that's draining.
- *Overindulging* by eating, drinking, or partying too much; binge-watching Netflix; buying things to a point where you get into debt.

- *Overdoing* exercise or physical labor that puts stress on the body, becoming a workaholic, sleeping too little to get something done or sleeping too much and getting nothing done.

Occasionally we might pull an all-nighter to get something done, binge watch a favorite show, get drunk at a party, take a break from work, or stop talking to someone we love when they get too draining. *Needing* to do things like this too often or doing them chronically as a coping mechanism can deplete you on a soul level. Feeding the ego does not sustain a sense of recharge nor does it feed the soul.

In essence, when nurturing the ego, you will notice what's going on around you as a justification for what you do. It might be a reactive impulse you indulge. It might be something you do that feels good in the moment, but it usually brings regret later.

After doing these things you may not notice your feelings—especially the uncomfortable ones. At best all you may achieve is to escape your cares for a period of time. Yet, no matter how long the escape, it often doesn't feel long enough before you have to reface your work and/or life challenges. When we nurture the ego, we often fail to evoke a sense of bonding with others in a meaningful way. There is a way to nurture the ego that does not bring the risk of harm or regret later.

Nurturing the Soul

When we nurture our soul, we often experience something more like a transformed or fresh perspective for something that challenges us. We feel more balanced, secure, and brave as we face our challenges. Feeding the soul feeds the ego too.

> Feeding the soul feeds the ego too.

Remember, as the ego seeks justification, the soul seeks validation. In essence, the ego has you looking outside yourself for relief, reason, motivation, and reward. On the contrary, the soul has you look within yourself for relevance, meaning, authenticity, and benefit for all. The soul has you notice (not judge) what's going on around you and observe (not judge) the effects on yourself. This includes observing what you think, what you feel, and how you act. The things you do for yourself are tools to restore your true nature no matter what is happening around you. Again, the soul does not judge itself or others. Nurturing the soul sustains a sense of recharge to face your challenges over a period of time.

When we nurture the soul we find our sense of self freely; our stamina for caring for ourselves and others while facing challenges feels more effortless and doable. Love, possibility, and joy become the means of establishing connection with others.

Let's look at personal power practice strategies that might appeal to your soul as well as your ego. Remember, what you do to nurture your soul also nurtures your ego.

To start, look at your list of Twenty-Five Things that bring you a sense of peace, fulfillment, happiness, confidence, energy, and/or growth. Cross off anything that involves any of the seven deadly sins. You will know they involve the seven deadly sins if by doing them you have ever observed yourself experiencing anything less than joy for having done them. Even though something might feel good, if it evokes guilt, shame, or any degree of self-loathing during or after the fact, scratch it off your list. You can replace it with something better.

You can read through the upcoming chapter(s) for lots of ideas to add to your list of Twenty-Five Things that you would like to try for nurturing and restoring your soul. Add any strategies that feel right for you. Do this now so that the next time you are experiencing overwhelm, exhaustion, cynicism, and powerlessness, you will have a list of options to choose from for the Engage phase of *the OPEN Method*. What you ultimately want is a list of things that you know you enjoy AND their practice leaves you fulfilled on a soul level.

It may seem like there are a lot of ideas—too many to choose from. Don't think of the strategies as a plate full of too much food. Instead, see them as a buffet table full of options to satisfy your current appetite. I suggest you try one thing from any of the symptoms you may be experiencing. If exhaustion is your primary concern, try one strategy from chapter 9. If it's cynicism, try one from chapter 10. If it's powerlessness, try one from chapter 11. If it's all three—exhaustion, cynicism, and powerlessness—try one from each of the next three chapters. If that feels like too much, try one from your top two symptoms. If the strategy doesn't work well for you, go back and try a different one. The best approach is to pick one that fits into your day, or into something you are dealing with at work right now. With practice, exhaustion can be returned to vigor, cynicism to civility, and powerlessness to a sense of personal power.

CHAPTER 9

ENGAGE—NURTURING STRATEGIES FOR VIGOR

Pivot from Exhaustion to Vigor

Remember the quote in chapter 5 from *A Course In Miracles* about inspiration versus fatigue? Let me refresh your memory:

> *The result of genuine devotion is inspiration, a word which properly understood is the opposite of fatigue. To be fatigued is to be dis-spirited, but to be inspired is to be in the spirit. To be egocentric is to be dis-spirited, but to be Self-centered in the right sense is to be inspired or in spirit.*

A Course in Miracles

This quote is relevant for exhaustion strategies that can replenish you on a soul level because exhaustion isn't simply being tired. Exhaustion at work primarily comes from being overwhelmed by your work or workload and losing a sense of connection with your work.[15] When we are overwhelmed by what we don't feel connected to, we can wonder who we are and what inspires us. Devotion brings inspiration—a key aspect for ascending from non-health-related fatigue. Devotion is defined as "profound dedication; consecration" and "earnest attachment to a cause, person." The quote from *A Course in Miracles* demonstrates a cause and effect relationship:

devotion ————————> inspiration

versus

dis-spirited ————————> fatigue

There may be things you think you are devoted to. But if a sense of inspiration is not experienced in return, are you truly devoted? Inspiration is not something you need to seek; it is a byproduct of your devotion, of your hope; and maybe of your courage. Another way to see devotion is to see it as honoring something. If you are experiencing exhaustion, ask yourself, "What have I been devoted to?"

Nurturing the soul during periods of exhaustion is about balancing out vigor-sucking conditions with vigor-giving conditions. As I said, I always tell my clients (and my kids) to follow a simple rule: Your personal power practice must be greater than or equal to the magnitude of feeling "I don't wanna … " about something you're about to experience. That means for every vigor-sucking experience you must endure, counterbalance it with a vigor-giving experience. It looks like this:

The Experience Spectrum

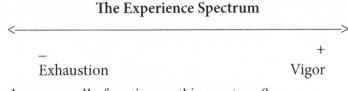

Where do you usually function on this spectrum?

Soul-Fulfilling Strategies during Times of Exhaustion

As I've explained, periods of exhaustion can be addressed by doses of medicine that restore your soul and enable vigor for you. Here are some suggestions.

Manage and Get Help with Your Workload

Workload has one of the strongest associations with job-related exhaustion. When managing and seeking help with your workload, it's important to have your boss's support. To do that, you will need to enlighten your boss about the state of your workload and its effect on you personally as well as professionally.

An effective way to educate your boss about your overwhelming workload is to get a list together of all the projects and regular tasks or responsibilities that are currently on your plate. To do this, I suggest you create a table or spreadsheet listing each project or responsibility down the first column. Then add additional columns for each of the following items.

Deadline: if there is a deadline, put the date in. If there isn't a deadline label it as ongoing.

Key Stakeholders: list who else contributes to producing work for the task or project. It's important to clarify roles as confusion over accountability often contributes to feeling depleted by your workload.

Resources: list the resources that are vital for productivity and meeting deadlines. This might include money, staff, equipment, authority, outside expertise, and more. Distinguish between those you have and those you don't yet have but require (you can do this with different colored or bolded text).

Status: keep this simple. Use green to show you're done; orange means you're working on it and it will be on time; yellow means you're working on it and there are obstacles to it getting done on time; red means it is stuck or stalled. If it's a routine responsibility then consider purple meaning ongoing and it's going smoothly; and blue meaning ongoing and it's *not* going smoothly. Of course, make up your own status codes so that it makes sense to you.

Priority: this means it is a *critical, high, medium,* or *low* priority that you personally work on this project or task with the workload you currently have. Often people think of priority as how important or near a deadline a task is. In the context of educating your boss about your state of overwhelm, *priority* is talking about talent resources. It's *critical* if only you have the necessary knowledge, expertise, talents, skills, and/or abilities for the task. It's *high* if you and only one other person has the ability to do the work. It's *medium* if there are a few people who have the ability, and it's *low* if many people have the ability to do the work.

Dedicated hours: note approximately how many hours a week each project or task requires of you. This includes time spent in meetings as well as time spent in actually working on the work.

Comments: this is where you explain status, and ask for what you require personally and professionally. This could include concerns you have with skill gaps, supportive relationships, flexibility, and better alignment of personal values and resources. If you don't know what you need, note that you require help to clarify obstacles and brainstorm options.

A simple one-page plan is all you need to serve as a tool to have a meaningful discussion with your boss. Often, bosses don't have a full picture of how the workload is building up or affecting their employees. Bosses tend to delegate without second guessing "yes, boss" answers. In my career I have often noticed that the most valued employees keep track of their work. In addition, they book time on their calendar for when they will do the work for the things they committed to in meetings, as well as for when they will attend meetings. When they are at capacity, they don't say "yes" or "no" to requests for additional work. Rather, they discuss with their boss what they already have going on and ask them which project or task their boss would prefer they put on hold or give to another employee. They use the word *required* versus words like *wanted* or *needed*. Often when employees use words like *want* or *need*, bosses may question the validity of such requests.

I know it may seem counterintuitive that a valued employee would put up what some might perceive as a roadblock to productivity. In reality, they are actually doing the opposite. They are performing as an expert of their profession. Experts always know what it will take to get something done well. Managing workload well is giving the people you serve insight into what it takes to get things done. It's giving them what director, screenwriter and actor Jim Jarmusch describes as *right, cheap,* or *fast* (pick two). It's important to collaborate with people and manage realistic expectations. The greater the gap between the demands of our workload and the rewards of our job, the more likely exhaustion can set in.

> The greater the gap between the demands of our workload and the rewards of our job, the more likely exhaustion can set in.

Advocate for Personal as well as Professional Resources

The two biggest influencers I have witnessed that shift people from working in closer alignment with a dimension of burnout to returning to engagement are resources and relationships. With managing workload, I offered you a way to talk with your boss about professional resources. Securing more reliable personal resources can also be a way to help you better with tight deadlines and the volume of work on the job.

More often in my private practice, I hear clients tell me about requiring personal resources just as much, if not more, than professional resources. Personal resources could be anything that enable you to attend your job and do your work. It might include more reliable transportation, work-from-home equipment, child or elder care, and help from partners or kids to keep up with daily and weekly household chores.

A way to get your arms around personal resource requirements is to write down what you are doing at home over the course of a week. That includes grooming; meal preparation and clean up; fitness; attending to children or other members of the household, the home, pets, finances, laundry, yard work. What are you spending your time on at home? When you have that list, write down the household member primarily accountable for each task. Are the responsibilities balanced? What is needed to make your home life run smoothly? Would it make a difference in your ability to be better engaged at your job if tasks were redistributed? Talk about the items that affect your job with your housemates and perhaps even your boss. As your housemates need to participate in a discussion to redistribute responsibilities at home, so does your boss need to participate in a discussion to redistribute responsibilities at your job. Share with both your housemates and your boss how things are affecting you personally and professionally. Make direct requests to start negotiations and be willing to listen and collaborate on designing alternative solutions.

Discover and Honor Your Boundaries and Values

Boundaries become clear when you are honest with what you observe about your thoughts, urges, and feelings. Instead of observing situations and other people, you can tune into your thoughts, urges, and feelings by asking, "When this situation shows up, what do I think; what do I wish to do or say? When someone does what that person who has me aggravated does, how do I feel?" The answer to these modified questions from the Observe step gives you insight into your boundaries.

Another way to know your boundaries is to understand your values. A value is something you appreciate as it makes it easier for you to do what you do to bring meaning to yourself and others. Honoring your values is a way to take care of yourself and communicate what matters most to you so that you can do what you are meant to do for others. There are three things you can do easily to practice boundaries around a value you hold. To begin, describe a value you hold in one word or a short phrase. I will use the example of *camaraderie* or *team-work* to demonstrate:

1. **Enable** your value. Ask yourself, "What would my value word do in this situation?" So if your value word is *camaraderie*, and you get a new project at work, you might answer this question by taking time to identify and include key stakeholders. It might simply be to invite different people to lunch or coffee, to get to know people at the beginning of the project.

2. **Advocate** for your value. Ask yourself, "What could others do to support me in experiencing my value word?" So again, if your value word is *camaraderie*, you might ask others to include you in events.

3. **Exercise** boundaries around that value. Exercising boundaries is sharing with others your ideas or concerns about your value word. Using the same example of *camaraderie*, you might suggest—to those who seem to overlook *camaraderie*—that others be invited. You might go so far as to share that you are not okay with what feels like to you a missed opportunity to build *camaraderie* among stakeholders. However far you take it, be sure you do it from a place that feels right for you versus judging others. When you observe your thoughts, urges, and feelings, the boundary to communicate might be obvious—especially from your feeling word(s). For example, if you are clear about the feeling of being *drained* from a perceived lack of *camaraderie* at your job, the boundary becomes easy to communicate. It could be conveyed like this: "It's not a good time to discuss this as I am feeling *drained* (convey your feeling word). Can I let you know when I feel ready to talk about it?"

Avoidance alone is not exerting a boundary. Exercising your boundaries calmly and without judgment is how conscious evolvement happens. It's also a way we teach others how to treat us. When people know what we can be counted on for, they tend to seek us out for that. When we avoid, others learn nothing about the boundary we want to enable. Therefore, they tend to keep coming back to us with the same crap we want no part of. In the process of avoidance, all we enable is a *whole lotta awkward*!

Create "Values Experiences"

Another way to explore your values is to create what I call "values experiences." It's something I do to nurture myself through periods of exhaustion and even cynicism. I simply choose a word that describes a quality that I value and would like to turn up the volume on noticing, practicing, and experiencing. I always believe this quality—this value—is already around me; I just might be too drained to notice it. So I decide that I will recognize and experience it in a more vivid way instead of focusing on what drains me. Remember, a value is something you appreciate as it makes it easier for you to do what you do to bring meaning to yourself and others. It could be a quality like beauty, cleanliness, order, fun, kindness.

Although you don't need others to provide your values for you, you express gratitude when others enable them for you. Noticing your values alive and well at your job enables you to offer your knowledge, skills, abilities, and talents more easily and with energy, no matter what is happening around you. Your values are also what you ask for and are on the lookout for from your job and your day in general.

I even like to choose a new word every year as an alternative to making new year resolutions. One year my word was *wonderful*. And that year I had a pretty darn wonderful year! I didn't accomplish all the to-dos I would have liked, and a lot of unexpected things came up, which could have easily been labeled as tough, heavy, or downright dark. Yet it was still a wonderful year. With everything that came up I would simply ask myself, *How can I bring the power of wonderful to this moment?* and it would be so that I was on my way to seeing and taking advantage of opportunities to experience more wonderfulness.

For example,

- I cleared some emotional blocks from my life PLUS I did it in Sedona, AZ. *Wonderful!*
- I changed up my health and fitness routine, rising at 4 a.m. most mornings to accomplish it. There is peace and solitude at the Jesus hour, PLUS I did it with friends and with amazing support from professionals. *Wonderful!*
- I started yoga with some meditation PLUS I did it with my husband and children, which made it a gift that became profoundly more *wonderful.*

I could go on and on with more examples but I hope you see what I mean. I never set out that year to change my fitness routine to include friends or trainers or go to Sedona, AZ in any way. I simply asked, *How can I bring the power of wonderful to this moment?* Sometimes I tailor that question to the situation. For example, I might alter the question to *What would make today more wonderful?* Or *What would make facing this problem wonderful?* Or *What would make preparing dinner more wonderful?* Sometimes what came to me was to just light a candle while making dinner. Other times I booked a trip to Sedona to heal some emotional trauma and was there two weeks later. One evening I said yes to an invite from a friend to check out an introduction seminar to a gym my friend wanted to join. And at that meeting I saw the possibility of community, support, and training my brain to think a different way, all things I believed would be *wonderful* enhancements to my fitness routine.

Process the world you find yourself in through the filter of your value experience. An easy way I create a value experience filter is by adopting a mantra—a set phrase or question to bring a mindful state about the value you choose to experience more vividly. My mantra as a phrase is *I can't wait to see how [INSERT YOUR VALUE WORD HERE] prevails!* As I explained earlier, I challenge myself to focus on how I can bring my value word to a situation. My mantra in the form of a question could be *How can I bring the power of [INSERT YOUR VALUE WORD HERE] to this moment?* For example, if *happiness* were my chosen quality or state of being, my mantra phrase would be *I can't wait to see how happiness prevails!* As a question it would be *How can I bring the power of happiness to this moment?* So when I'm feeling drained or crabby, I simply turn to the mantra phrase or question to process my world through a possibility I value.

The soul will offer this word to others as well. It will ask, *How can I bring the experience of happiness to this person or situation?* The soul waits for an answer to surface and takes action on that answer. If no answer surfaces, it trusts there is nothing more for you to do except be present, listen, and ask the question again when another question, offer, or request, is directed your way.

Choose a value experience. Maybe it's a value that you acknowledge already having, yet would like to experience more vividly. Make yourself accountable for choosing *what shall be* and allow God or the energy of the universe to provide *how it shall be*. Giving yourself an experience to drop accountability for *how* and only focusing on *what* is an easy way to experience lightening the load you might feel. It can also teach you how much a shift in your energy brings opportunities and experiences you desire *to you*—you don't have to chase after everything all the time.

Offer versus Give

Often we are exhausted because we put a skewed sense of responsibility on ourselves. One of the most powerful concepts I have taught clients that makes a difference for what they say "takes a weight off their shoulders" is the concept of *offer* versus *give*.

Giving is predicated on receiving. You don't really "give" unless another "receives" and hopefully receives well. *Giving* may also be a concept of going out and getting something you don't already have in order to give it away.

Merriam-Webster defines these two terms as follows:

Give—"to grant or bestow by formal action; to put into the possession of another for his or her use; to yield possession of by way of exchange"

Offer—"to present as an act of worship or devotion; to present for acceptance or rejection; to propose or suggest; to make available"

Offering is predicated on soul-validating service. It's *offering* others things you already have, such as your talents, skills, knowledge, and abilities. You serve aspects of yourself only to the capacity that you actually have them. It does not serve another to *offer* or *give* something if it means a detriment to yourself or others.

Offering is also about allowing the other to accept your offer—or not. Securing a sense of clarity, confidence, and conviction for your work has nothing to do with whether or how others receive you. In *offering*, we must detach from potential results or rewards that could be possible if the offer were to be received. *Offering* requires us to surrender to an experience of rejection without making another's preference (or readiness) mean anything about us or what we have to offer.

We can never be ready to work with a sense of purpose and connection to our calling when we are focused on serving everyone we interact with flawlessly. Or when we are focused on what we might receive in return for having served. Soul fulfillment and working with a sense of purpose come from *offering* what we have to offer. This is done regardless of whether or not the people we serve shower us with gratitude or we get the results we ultimately strive to achieve. Of course, life at work is much sweeter when we win adoration and rewards and hit our targets. But being adored, paid, and meeting goals alone do not guarantee a lasting sense of fulfillment. Do they? The workforce is full of achieving, paid people who are adored yet still unhappy (as much as 70 percent of the workforce, as a matter of fact).

When the ego is in charge of serving others, it unwittingly does so from a place of *giving*. That leaves you on the lookout for whether or not the *giving* is deserved or aptly appreciated. Is it a mystery how or why exhaustion (and no doubt cynicism) sets in?

Egos must be fed, so *giving* is an act of the ego since it requires another's receipt plus something in return, even if it's just a "thank you." In giving, we can become highly offended if the person won't take our service and won't give something back in return. Did you ever get offended when someone didn't say, "Thank you"?

If we perceive that we might lose in some way, say, if our service is not regarded well or reciprocated appropriately, we are more likely to withhold our talents, abilities, and knowledge. It's exhausting to withhold what's natural for us to offer. Ever lose business to someone else? We likely want to know, *Why not work with me? What do they have that I don't have?*

There's an entitlement that comes from *giving*. Even if it's just a feeling that we did something good, such as when we do a favor for someone or donate time or money to a charity. In business, we might expect favors to be returned in the future, such as through a connection on LinkedIn at the very least, and the expectation of loyalty or reciprocity of some kind in the future—for sure! When we hold unfulfilled entitlements we nurture a mindset aligned with burnout.

When we serve from a place of *offering*, we expect nothing in return. Offering is an act of the soul. The power of offering comes from within and does not require another's acceptance or approval to be complete. In offering, not only do we leave the recipient free to decide whether they want what we are offering, we are also less likely to consider whether or not someone is deserving of what we have to offer. With that, we are less likely to withhold our gifts. It's easier to be who we are despite what is happening around us when we have no need for others to behave in a certain way. In *giving*, our job is done only when another receives (and receives well); in *offering*, our job is done once we make an offer. With offering, we are making a choice to be in our innate ability to have the power of God or the universe coming through us. The return for this choice to offer without expectation of anything in return is that it always puts us in alignment with feeling connected to a sense of purpose.

When people sense a demand is dressed in only the clothing of offering, they tend to feel pushed and they usually will push back or resist altogether. Genuine offers (which include a willingness to experience some variation of "No" as an answer) are often also sensed and tend to evoke cooperation.

Consider how Jesus practiced offering. "And the power of the Lord was with Jesus to heal the sick."[16] Christ didn't take time to get to know the sick person and judge whether or not they deserved healing. He just offered healing. Why? It wasn't for followers, money, a promotion, fame, a positive review, a testimonial, a "Like" on social media, or a thank-you note. He did it simply because it was what He was here to do. It fulfilled his soul and kept Him on his path of purpose.

Do you do what you are here to do without regard for what you will get in return? Or do you gauge and hold back if you don't perceive what's in it for you? If you hold back, you might be in alignment with *giving* versus *offering*, exhaustion, and with a path to burnout versus a path of purpose. With the ego and giving, we become the cumulation of the ten people we hang out with the most. We want what they want and become convinced we should be content to be no better than them. It's like having to get dressed in the morning using other people's toiletries and clothing where nothing fits or works for us quite as well as our own toiletries and clothing. We must maintain favor in order to fit in and feel valued.

> When we are in service to what we believe would make a difference for others, we are required only to offer what we have to offer and allow others to be free to accept our offering or not, without judgment or punishment.

The soul and offering maintain their sense of power and allow others to do the same. When we are in service to what we believe would make a difference for others, we are required only to offer what we have to offer and allow others to be free to accept our offering or not, without judgment or punishment. The bonus on top when we offer our best to others is we enable a spirit of cooperation into the situation. Be willing to show others something you know or can do that you believe can offer value to them, and allow them to decide whether they are interested and ready to receive it or not. You stay humble by allowing the other person's ego the freedom to say, "No, you idiot, leave me alone!" Instead, you're more likely to hear some variation of, "Thank you and it's not right for me" or "Thank you and I am not ready to experience or receive that."

People sense when they are truly free to say "yes" or "no" without judgment or potential problems. People know when they are in the presence of a "command" wrapped up as though it were a choice. How do you react when you sense you don't really have a choice? How do you react when you sense you really do have a choice? Which scenario leaves you feeling more open and willing to say "yes"—open to collaborating and finding common ground so everyone can feel good about the situation? People love feeling free to receive or not receive what we offer them. When people feel a true spirit of freedom, they often are more open to cooperating or to at least joining you in negotiating for a win-win solution. Inspiring civility, cooperation, collaboration, and energy is no more complicated than offering what you have to offer and allowing "no" as a possible response, without making it mean anything about you or the other person.

Even if someone doesn't want what we have to offer, we can maintain dignity and self-respect because we did our work, which was to make the offer no matter what's happening around us. There's no power in creating a pretense that you could take away another's opportunity for choice—you can't. Choice that enables acceptance and peace to prevail is an act of the soul. There's no need to pressure a favorable choice from another unless we wish to align ourselves with pressure and judgment for our choices. Your power does not come from people taking what you have to offer or from getting the results you seek. Your power comes from offering what you have to offer no matter how another is behaving, and from advocating for what will most easily enable you to offer what you offer, while allowing the results to be what they will be.

The energy of the universe loves an open, humble soul and ego working together because energy flows where there is an opportunity for it to flow. It will favor flowing toward truth (soul-centered offerings). In the absence of humble truth, energy will flow where it most believes it is entitled to be received (the biggest ego in the room).

When it comes to experiencing inspiration and vigor from our jobs, we must switch from holding ourselves accountable for *giving* and move toward *offering*. The truth is the only giving we can ever feel a sense of power from is when we *give to (and receive from) ourselves*. With everyone else, our true power is experienced in what we *offer*, never in what we receive.

Disengagement and the path to burnout may be more likely with an ego-centered (a.k.a.—quid pro quo) approach to work:

You give + they receive = they give you something in return + you become energized

Or

You give + they receive = they don't give you something in return + you become drained

Or

You give + they don't receive = you become quickly drained

Engagement and the path of purpose may be more likely with a soul-fulfilling approach to work:

You offer what you have to offer + they do or don't receive = they are as open to collaborating with you as they possibly can be + you maintain your power

When we think what's happening around us is justification for not being ourselves or offering our best service, we detach from a sense of purpose. And when we don't receive what we value in return for our service, we get really detached really fast. Holding yourself account-able for *offering* versus *giving* safeguards you from perceiving that others hold power over you. During times of exhaustion, we must switch our focus from what we *give* to what we *offer*.

The essence of explaining the concept of *offering* versus *giving* is explained in a well-known adage. Did you ever hear, "You can lead a horse to water but you can't make him drink"? You are *offering* when you inform another (such as telling a horse about the best water you know) and suggest taking them there. Now this is where a lot of people go wrong and unwittingly blur their connection with their purpose. To believe it's your job to convince the horse to accept your offer plus drink the water AND it's the horse's job to appreciate it is *giving*! In *giving*, we *tell, direct,* and *imply* an expectation of reciprocity. We, consciously or subconsciously, must have the horses in our life agree they need water AND that they need to be taken to it, by you, of course. In return, they need to cherish us for doing that—otherwise we didn't do a valid job or we didn't "work hard enough." We might even think we could have and should have done better.

You might think, *If I were more credentialed, experienced, polished, connected, blah, blah, blah—then they would have taken it and praised me for it!* To cope with these uncomfortable, and possibly subconscious thoughts and feelings, we project them outward. The behavior we then notice in others around us becomes uninspiring and leaves us depleted.

Relax

Plan time to detach from work (and anything that drains you). This means planning for deliberate fun; indulging your interests and curiosity, and exploring things that ignite inspiration, passion, beauty, peace, or excitement within you. This includes turning off your cellphone and computer. That means no email, social media, or apps, including games. Instead, deliberately do something relaxing. It's not about doing nothing. No energy in equals no energy out. Make this time conscious and planned, like a meeting you have scheduled with yourself for physical and emotional recovery. This may also be a great time to do something from your list of Twenty-Five Things!

Time off should never feel like a burden. Time off is time to reconnect with yourself—mind, body, and soul—and avoid anything that drains or distracts you. It is ideal if you can take twenty-four hours a week to be the creator of your own joy. I make six days a week about the things I "have to" get done and one day a week simply about nurturing my soul. Time off sometimes includes a planned nap; doing something fun I like to do; giving extra time to my family, friends, or pets; organizing some space in my home; watching a movie in the middle of the day; or visiting places I think are beautiful. On occasion, I even enjoy doing things I enjoy most for my work. On that day off I notice that I often reflect on how much I actually enjoy "getting stuff done" such as working, managing personal finances, running errands, cleaning, and even doing laundry. I have found that my seventh day ritual is a day when I plan what I choose to do. I do it for my soul restoration and nurturance not necessarily to *get something done I've been meaning to get done for a long time* not unless getting it done would be a joy. It's about exploration of what enriches my soul. It's a day of putting the full power of my awesomeness in my own corner. On my seventh day, there is no "have to"; there is only "want to." Removing the "have to" factor has taught me that things are only a drag when I label them with "have to."

Define your own "Sabbath"—a time to go within, purge built-up exposure to things that drain you, and discover what feeds your soul.

CHAPTER 10

ENGAGE—NURTURING STRATEGIES FOR CIVILITY

Pivot from Cynicism to Civility

A study found that there is a correlation between cynical attitudes and being at greater risk for cardiovascular disease.[17] Sadly, however, as of the time of the writing of this book, there has not yet been sufficient research and study about interventions designed to change cynical attitudes and whether such changes would alter health risks. Another study shows that cynicism alone may be more indicative of burnout evolving over time than exhaustion or powerlessness.[18] I am not a researcher, but I have observed and learned from those I have coached that a changed perspective can often lead to lasting behavioral and emotional shifts in our disposition.

Cynicism is rooted in judgment that comes from being distrustful. When we have a cynical attitude, we fear that our point of view, boundaries, and contributions won't be respected or valued. It is a reaction of the ego that seeks justification to feel respected and valued. Civility is a response of the soul and is an authentic expression rooted in what you wish to create despite what's happening around you. Although we

171

cannot ultimately control how others will treat, react, or respond to us, we can control how we treat and respond to others, and how we treat and respond to ourselves. It's all about respectful interactions whether or not we agree with their approaches, ideas about what it takes to get the job done well, or values.

Look, we all have our off days. We can have our moods from time to time but what we cannot do is sustain a sense of satisfaction from our work if we indulge our reactive moods. At work, our moods tend to become reactive when we are focused on less-than-favorable external factors that on the surface seem to only promise aggravation versus rewards. This includes experiencing depleting activities such as these without trust that we will restore ourselves:

- doing stuff we don't like to do,
- worrying about how other people may react to what we do or say,
- interacting with people we don't like or don't share relatedness with,
- having to do more with less time and resources,
- having to go somewhere we don't like to go,
- working under undesirable conditions.

Often, we may feel that we have little to no control over how such situations might play out.

Soul-Fulfilling Strategies during Times of Cynicism

If work has you feeling like a walking, breathing eye roll, shift your focus to soul-fulfilling approaches. The following are a few suggestions.

Socialize Inside and Outside of Work

One of the most important things you can do to recover or safeguard yourself from cynicism is to make meaningful connections with others.

As I said before, the two biggest influencers I have witnessed that shift people from working in closer alignment with a dimension of burnout to returning to engagement are resources and relationships. Now let's look at relationships.

With my clients and the employees I have witnessed in performance counseling, when I worked in my corporate role, people who have been perceived to be cynical often point to relationships somehow being at the root cause of their attitude on the job. This may look like a lack of teamwork, camaraderie, and social support within the work environment. It also might be a perceived or actual conflict of values. During times of cynicism, it is important to build and keep strong relationships around you. Build them at work, and keep the fulfilling relationships you have outside of work strong. If you don't have any close relationships or co-workers, you can find support among your family, friends, neighbors, mentors, teachers, and peers. They are the people you know or meet through work, school, religious affiliations, in volunteering for charities, or in organizations that are of interest to you.

The way to build new relationships and keep established ones healthy is the same—*do stuff* together. Here's what I mean.

When socializing during times of cynicism with the people who are part of your pack, tribe, network, circle of friends and family, or whatever you call those who you already know and love, be sure they are people who fill you up. When you do get together, be sure you are talking about experiences of peace, fulfillment, happiness, confidence, conviction, and growth, in addition to challenges. This isn't the time to rehash what your jerky boss did or said to you or to anyone else. Chat about things that would be on the hope end of the Faith Spectrum. It's okay to share something upsetting that happened to you; just be sure to also share how you are nurturing yourself through such challenges. Make the main point of what you are saying be what you observed about yourself and how you are feeling about what happened, versus rehashing what happened and who is to blame.

It's also important to spend time with your work peers—even the ones that annoy you from time to time. The criteria for bonding with those who nurture your soul doesn't require you to find or align with people who always agree with you. Establishing connection must include doing fun things outside the work environment with the people you work with versus leaving all your interactions to be formed in the context of your job. People bond quickly when they get to see a side of you they don't normally see. If it's someone at work who bugs you, consider allowing them to see your relaxed, fun side and offer yourself the opportunity to see that side of them. When you are hanging out with people from work, leave work at work. If they want to bring things up, listen without any pressure of responding or making any commitments. I know this step may seem strange with work people who may deplete you, but socializing by *doing* something (versus just gossiping, complaining, or eating) can restore and nurture your soul. It puts the focus on what you are doing instead of how you make each other feel. It builds memories and gives you a shifted perspective of another—and them of you. You don't have to make your social interaction long. Even just a walk to your car or sharing a zoom chat about a household repair or a sport your co-worker also enjoys for a few minutes after work can build the relationship.

Eating doesn't count for *doing* things together. It's nice to share a meal with people but eating, on its own, is not enough to build memories or ties that energize. Often, people will use food as a vice to soothe a wounded ego. So food doesn't count. An alternative to just eating together is to organize activities you enjoy and invite others to join you; consider a book club, a sports or game night, a musical jam session in your basement or garage, and movie nights to offer a few ideas.

The bottom line is, it's hard to feel like you fit into a work environment when you don't have any social connection with the people you work with. When we feel that we are working where we don't fit, our potential for work enjoyment and maintaining strong job performance can be at a higher risk of suffering. When we interact and connect with people we relate to or care about, it becomes really easy for us to do all we can to work well with them.

Connection also includes practicing empathy, which seeks to understand versus judging what might initially seem annoying. Especially in times of conflict, seek to understand first, and then seek to relate. Have you ever experienced anything similar? Offering empathy can be simple. A dear friend and work colleague of mine once referred to this as "assuming best intentions," while asking, "Would you be willing to help me understand your point of view?" Your empathy and pledge to be open to find a solution that works for both of you may be all it takes to ward off cynicism in yourself and others.

Resources for developing connection through improving relationships and how you communicate within your relationships may be realized in programs such as Landmark Education; Byron Katie's The Work; and *Nonviolent Communication*.

Learn About and Practice Positivity and Happiness

I once saw Oprah Winfrey interview Shawn Achor. Shawn is an expert in the study of positive psychology, which I was shocked to learn became a mainstream term in 1998.[19] Did the world really wait this long to talk about the effects of happiness and positivity?

In the interview, Shawn says something I have believed for years: lasting success follows happiness—never the other way around. In all my correspondence as a career coach, I typically sign off with, "Best wishes for your continued happiness and success." It's very deliberate that happiness is before success in that statement. When we know what is easy for us to offer, we feel happy to offer it. Offering it enables rewards that validate our soul and ego. Often, rewards received through alignment with the soul are experienced as feelings such as peace, joy, love, gratitude, and generosity. The result of those feelings often fuels our capacity for happiness and fulfillment, which leads to engagement and ego-nurturing rewards that symbolize success (e.g., money and recognition).

When we forgo personal clarity of understanding what we have to offer, or we hold back on offering our knowledge, skills, and talents, we are vulnerable to chasing rewards that only satisfy the ego. Rewards of the ego are material at best and experienced as intellectual justifications for what we have, want, do, and for what others will get from us. We have a choice: (1) to focus on seeking rewards that can only justify the ego or (2) to focus on seeking rewards that validate the soul while also receiving the byproduct material rewards that satisfy the ego.

> We have a choice: (1) to focus on seeking rewards that can only justify the ego or (2) to focus on seeking rewards that validate the soul while also receiving the byproduct material rewards that satisfy the ego.

Anyway, Shawn offered five simple things you can practice to experience a richer, more sustainable sense of happiness. Of course, I went right to work on them.

1. **Every morning, name three things you are grateful for.** My young daughter and I used to share a morning cuddle every day and discuss our three things. Then I would text each of our three things to my husband and son, and they would share back their three things. This is a great exercise during periods of cynicism.

2. **Every night, journal details about something meaningful you experienced in the past twenty-four hours.** As members of a family, we would each discuss this at dinner every night. Sometimes I would write about it in a journal I keep. I have noticed meaningful events come in the simplest ways, such as holding a door open for another, noticing someone going the extra mile for me, receiving a smile from a stranger, accepting money for the parking meter from a stranger, and acknowledging a compliment. This "meaningful" exercise would bring

each of us to a more present state for such moments. It would help us see the not-so-nice moments as our opportunities to enable the creation of a meaningful contribution.

3. **Every day, thank or acknowledge someone for something they did.** A simple text or email does it if you don't have the opportunity to say it in person. And it takes less than twenty seconds. Gratitude is easy and effective. It acknowledges what you value having available to you. A word of thanks teaches people how they can support you. It demonstrates to God and the energy of the universe (or whatever you believe in) what you would like more of in your life. It's also a simple act that can help train your brain and direct your ego about what to be on the lookout for.

4. **Exercise.** As often as you can, take time to exercise. It trains your brain to believe that your behavior matters. Move your body in a way that feels good. Whether that's walking, running, yoga, Pilates, strength training, or swimming. It could also be as simple as parking farther away from the building you work in, taking the stairs versus the elevator, or switching from meeting your friends for drinks once a week to meeting them at the gym at least once a week. You don't need a gym, new workout clothes, or hundreds of dollars' worth of personal coaching. Just do one thing in the name of your fitness such as taking a weekly walk, or doing some stretches while you watch a thirty-minute episode of your favorite sitcom. Reinforce what you do as exercise with gratitude for your body's ability to move and strengthen. Exercise is also an excellent way to restore vigor and confidence.

5. **Every day, meditate, pray, or just observe your breath.** Do whichever feels right for you. What matters is that you take as little as two minutes and as much as thirty minutes twice a

day or more to focus. Shawn says focusing on one thing for a period of time reduces stress.

Happiness is experienced in fleeting moments. Positive psychology research has found that only 10 percent of our long-term levels of happiness come from external factors (i.e., what others give or do for us), whereas 90 percent comes from how we naturally and deliberately process the world we find ourselves in.[20] Even though we may be born to naturally process the world in a more negative way, Marci Shimoff shares in her book, *Happy for No Reason: 7 Steps to Being Happy from the Inside Out*, that we can move our genetic "happiness set-point" through deliberate practice. Our happiness set-point is "the genetic and learned tendency to remain at a certain level of happiness, similar to a thermostat setting on a furnace."[21] That means that even though our DNA and environment may have a strong influence on the levels of happiness chemicals our brain produces, we can change it. We do that through the thoughts we think. And no doubt, through the feelings we nurture and the actions we take. That means we can learn to notice what leaves us feeling more optimistic and eventually become happier with practice.

Immerse yourself in what fills your energy or "follow your bliss," as Joseph Campbell, the prolific writer, editor, public speaker, and college professor, taught us. Honor that blissful experience by becoming conscious of it, nurturing it, and having gratitude for it. As a society we can do better at learning what positivity even is. Two of the most popular classes ever are Harvard University's *Positive Psychology* and Yale University's *Psychology and the Good Life*. People want to know if they can experience happiness despite their conditions. We can! It's not just about being nice, seeing the glass half full, or ignoring real things that are happening to us and draining us. A great place to start, for those of us who aren't into giving the time or money to enroll in ivy league courses, is to read *Happy for No Reason: 7 Steps to Being Happy from the Inside Out* by Marci Shimoff or anything written by Shawn Achor. To learn from a story perspective, try *The Alchemist* by Paulo Coelho or *God on a Harley* by Joan Brady.

Laugh

According to Psychology Today, there are four types of humor.[22] You want to use affiliative humor ONLY. Affiliative humor is G-rated humor—jokes about everyday life. It's humor that is *good clean fun*. Think about things you can laugh at with kids. I love to watch *Kid Snippets* online. They are short, funny videos of adults acting out scenarios imagined and narrated by kids—check them out! The other types of humor—aggressive humor, self-enhancing humor, or self-defeating humor—should be avoided. These types involve insults, put-downs, making yourself or someone else the target of the joke, and/or joking about bad things that have happened. These types of humor are best avoided while you are restoring your capacity for engagement. We cannot nurture ourselves on a soul level through exposure to content that includes disturbing images, bad news, or stimulates *the 7 deadlies* on any level. If you have to watch it, save that content for when you're in a restored mindset. I believe laughter is the greatest protection and game changer when you are facing anything that evokes fear (stress).

Practice Grace

One powerful antidote to cynicism may lie in working to improve your relationships through offering a civil approach toward others. Civility is easier with people you feel connected to so consider participating in opportunities to bond with others. Until you can build and establish relationships, another approach is to practice grace. I once had a co-worker who always seemed in a good mood. She regularly handled our sometimes jerky boss flawlessly. One day I asked her how she stayed so positive in his presence. She said, *"I kill 'em with kindness."* Some people do that unauthentically to just manipulate or placate another, but in her case I believed the kindness was genuine. It made no sense to me at the time, but now I get it. She was practicing grace, which is being kind to those who don't deserve it while doing what you can do for them.

The context of all service is forgiveness and grace. *Forgiveness* happens when we grant relief for another or for ourself. This relief can be from resentment, justified retaliation, or payment of something owed. *Grace* is unmerited favor. As we are all service providers, we can drive ourselves nuts if we were to consider whether everyone around us deserved our service. Doing so leads to cynicism. Often people are rude, fussy, irritated, annoyed, tired, or anxious when they are in need of something. Those behaviors and feelings don't often appeal to anyone, including to people who are equipped to make the pain of another go away. Forgiveness and grace, by design, are often undeserved, rarely can be earned, and when received are hard to pay back. If others are treating you badly and you react with more bad behavior (arguing, insults, defensiveness, finger-pointing), then you are bringing that energy into your life as well as enabling it in the world. If others treat you badly and you react in a civil way (connection, empathy, respect, and nurturing yourself), then you enable *that* energy in the world and certainly bring that energy into your life.

Grace puts you in control because it functions without dependence on how others are treating you. If you live your life believing no one is ever entitled to have a moment of poor character, you are going to live a very frustrating and lonely life. Although people are entitled to have *jerky* moments, it doesn't mean you have to be a jerk right back—even if it is justified. I suggest you have a simple plan for people having a *jerky* moment who come your way. An easy plan is to simply listen to understand the source of another's problem and offer them the help or support you actually have available. It doesn't mean opening a vein and letting a vampire feed.

Grace includes three elements:

1. listening versus reacting emotionally—convey understanding for another versus persuading them to your point of view,
2. offering your best service and attitude while keeping your boundaries intact—it's never about making yourself vulnerable in any way,
3. apologizing for any misunderstanding or miscommunication—leave out justifying why you did or said anything you may have done or said—it only evokes defensiveness.

Offering these three elements are going to seriously change the situation—even for the biggest, baddest attitude directed right at you. TRY IT!

Secure Clarity for What Is Wanted versus Unwanted

As I introduced in chapter 5, civility can be restored by asking yourself, *What would be the opposite of what I don't want to do, what I wish to avoid, and/or what I am afraid of?*

An exercise I do with clients who struggle with cynicism is to encourage them to notice the cynical language they use. They can replace cynical words that they say to themselves and out loud with language that's more aligned with civility. Such cynical language typically includes words such as *don't, won't, can't, should, shouldn't, have, but, without, not, need,* and *want.* These words come from a context of what isn't wanted or is perceived to be lacking. Use of them only manifests more of *what isn't wanted* and/or *is lacking.*

Language that promotes civility typically includes words such as *will, and, with, have.* So if what they want is *teamwork,* but what they notice and speak about is filled with cynical language (i.e. *this team can't work well together*), I ask them to say to themselves, "Wait, erase that. Instead, I'm so grateful for all the *teamwork* I experience each day. I can't wait to see how *teamwork* will prevail even though I notice and

fear more *dysfunction and back-stabbing."* The first and second reference is to what you are grateful for and what you want; they may even
be value words. The third reference is what you already regretfully
notice, such as perceived obstacles and limitations that you prefer to
avoid experiencing any further.

Clarity for what you want is easy and effective. It doesn't negate
anything currently happening or anything that may have happened in the past. It just shifts you to focus on what you want to
experience.

Notice your doubt, worry, fear, and guilt-filled thoughts. They
are all just possible visions for the future in the same way that hope
is just a possible vision for the future too. What matters is the vision
you choose to give your attention to. Acknowledge that your ego was
in the driver's seat as evidenced by your cynical language. Thank it
because its intent was to protect you. Plus it provides powerful velocity for figuring out what you *do* want. Then evolve the cynical words
or phrases into what promotes civility and clarity for what is wanted.
Doing so strengthens your ability to notice and act on opportunities
that reinstate your soul to the driver's seat and get you back on the
path of purpose.

Be Supportive and Helpful

Being supportive does not mean being someone people can complain
to or turn their problems over to. Offering support just means being
there and listening without judgment. Listen by repeating back what
you hear, and asking questions about the thoughts, urges, and feelings
that were evoked from what was experienced. Helping means asking,
"What would make a difference for you right now?" Whether you are
asking this question of yourself or another you are helping, this question
is about deciding what would make facing a challenge more tolerable.
Answering it is making an active choice to restore the power of the soul.
It's not always about solving the problem. I believe things either change

on their own or they never change at all. When you or another is in a state of cynicism, it's better to identify what one or two things would enable acceptance of the situation or solutions to address the situation to emerge. You want solutions that surface from a state of care, calm, and clarity. In essence, you are beginning the process of opening up clarity for what is wanted (versus what is unwanted). Often when we are depleted, cynical, or feeling powerless, it can be hard to know what we want. It can be easier to know one or two things that would make the situation feel more tolerable. Don't think beyond two things as anything more can feel like a chore, plus it just gets too far into the future.

It's time to focus on what you can do to be supportive and helpful for yourself and others. *Give* yourself support and *offer* support to others without concern for what you will get in return, either good or bad. That is taking your power back and that is the path of purpose.

CHAPTER 11

ENGAGE—NURTURING STRATEGIES FOR PERSONAL POWER

Pivot from Powerlessness to Personal Power

Powerlessness is a reduced ability to address, manage, or get done what has meaning to you. It is marked by a diminished morale and feeling you are ineffective at your job because you are depleted of personal power, confidence, control, or resources. As individuals, we, as employees, cannot control how much an organization will get involved and deal with what is contributing to us feeling powerless to perform. We can only focus on what we can do to help ourselves not fall victim to feeling powerless. And there is some good news in that because even when being supportive and helpful, an employer's efforts will never be more powerful than what employees can do for themselves to become engaged and connected to a sense of purpose with their work.

Soul-Fulfilling Strategies during Times of Powerlessness

Here are some strategies you may want to add to your *Personal Power Practice* for restoring your sense of power and enabling a soul-fulfilled approach to work.

Develop Your Skills and Self-Esteem

Self-esteem is feeling clarity and confidence about ourselves and having the conviction to offer our best to others. Internal esteem is sustainable esteem, meaning how we define and meet our own standards of value and self-worth matter more than relying primarily on others to show us respect and regard. When others compliment and value us, it can be wonderful, but we cannot primarily define our worth based on compliments from others.

Developing and practicing self-esteem can be as simple as

- defining and living by your values,

- learning to observe, acknowledge, forgive, and accommodate your weaknesses or faults,

- switching from a *giving*-based manner of service to an *offering*-based manner of service.

It can also be accessible by reading self-help books, working with a life or career coach, investing in behavioral therapy, or taking classes around skills you are interested to develop and practice. It can also be as simple as learning and practicing meditation especially if coping with the conditions of your job or life are challenging at this time. There are tons of options for courses through a google search for *meditation, personal development, personal growth, self-improvement,* or *self-esteem.* The range of topics is vast and include popular options such as developing skills in leadership, communication or public speaking, critical thinking, confidence, life mastery, and time management, to name few. A favorite resource I recommend is the American Management Association at www.amanet.org.

If investing hundreds of dollars isn't an option you are comfortable with right now, then you can do some work around connecting with your best talents. Let go of the idea that your best talents are those related to sports or artistic abilities. Your best talents are most likely better than being TV-worthy; they are more likely to be making-a-meaningful-difference-worthy.

A way to get in touch with your best talents is to ask yourself these questions and hear your own answers deeply:

- "What do I intend for others?"
- "What do I do better than most people?"
- "How do I make a difference for others?"
- "What would my closest relatives or friends say I do well (even though I might not agree with them)?"

Identify the behaviors or beliefs that might be holding you back from connecting with what you do to create meaningful differences for others. Offering your best to others is key to expanding your sense of self-esteem and accomplishment.

If there is any aspect of your job that you don't feel qualified to do, consider investing in developing that skill. I know some employers may not be very generous with how much they will pay for development opportunities but it's simply something you must invest in yourself if they will not pay for it. The longer and more rigorously you invest in being a student of your profession, the more powerful and valuable you become to your profession. Another benefit of continued learning and growing is that it keeps your brain strong and healthy.

Accommodate Your Weaknesses

Another opportunity for esteem development isn't just in discovering and embracing your strengths, it's also in discovering, owning, and accommodating your weaknesses. Accommodating my weaknesses was an area of self-esteem development that really challenged me. That was back when I tended to make decisions with more consideration for my judgments. I had a long history of judging, analyzing, and pushing myself to make tough decisions a lot—actually—to death. It was a fear-based way of life for me for a very long time. Just ask anyone in my family or any of my friends. My husband and kids might tell you I still do it from time to time.

That's the thing about who we are. No matter what we learn, or where we go, or who we interact with, there we are. My tendency to make decisions and then analyze them or plan for how I would deal with anything that could possibly go wrong made me an effective human resources executive. I could figure out approaches that could work in matters that affected a lot of people. Often these situations involved emergencies, multiple parties who each had conflicting values, resource constraints, economic pressures, and legal compliance considerations. However, not knowing when to shut off that superpower also brought a lot of "things going wrong" into my life. That was a time in my life I now affectionately refer to as the working-along-the-path-to-burnout years.

Learning to forgive and even embrace this superpower of mine (which will never go away) enabled me to discern when it's prudent to use my ability to see what could go wrong, weigh the pros and cons, and put safeguards in place to handle potential problems. When this urge to analyze, judge, and plan for potential catastrophe comes up, I embrace it. I recognize the value it *can* bring when used in the right context. However, I have also learned to assess when indulging that urge can slow down and cloud my ability to recognize clarity for what I want to vividly experience.

Please, notice, own, and accommodate yourself for your weaknesses. Your weaknesses aren't really weaknesses—they are strengths with undisciplined fear energy attached to them. Natural aptitudes or talents expressed through fear and the ego are weaknesses or they can express as strengths that leave collateral damage. Natural aptitudes or talents

> Please, notice, own, and accommodate yourself for your weaknesses.

expressed through hope and the soul are strengths that don't leave collateral damage. In essence, there is very little we do that is purely "good" or "bad"—there is a circumstance under which just about every human ability can add value.

When our tendencies are expressed for the benefit of the self (ego), they tend to eventually lead us into trouble and burnout over time. When they are expressed for the benefit of service to others (soul), they will be expressed as benefit to all; they will keep us connected to purpose. Your "weaknesses" are part of your personality, and from them you have an opportunity to practice nurturing yourself. Your expression of your personality, talents, knowledge, skills, abilities, experience, personal and professional boundaries, and capacity to be supportive and helpful to others comes from your soul. A way to build your "soul muscle" is to own and accommodate your weaknesses.

Strengths tend to make things happen easily, weaknesses slow progress down. Most people can easily think of a weakness they have, because weaknesses typically have some past suffering attached to them. Think of a subject you didn't do well at in school, something you don't like to do. We tend not to like what we don't think we can do well. Think of something that you struggled to accomplish.

Here is a template to help you develop your self-esteem muscle for your weaknesses: *A weakness I have is* _____. *What I have learned to do to accommodate myself with that weakness is*

_____.

I had a client once say their weakness was always being late or forgetting appointments. I will call her Zoe. She would often get lost in her work; time just didn't matter once she got in that zone. Looking at this, Zoe could see the beauty of having the ability to get lost in her work. The price she paid for that superpower, when she allowed it to be expressed through fear, the ego, or subconsciously, was being late or forgetting appointments. Aside from being viewed in various negative ways by those she had the appointments with, doing nothing about a tendency for lateness depleted Zoe's capacity for engagement in her work. How she learned to accommodate herself with that weakness was to keep an organized calendar and set alarms on her smartphone a few minutes before she had to leave so she could comfortably transition out of head-down work mode and get to her appointment on time.

Owning your weaknesses and accommodating yourself demonstrate your choice to live and work in alignment with your soul—and be on the path of purpose. This choice is powerful because it has consciousness attached to it. Getting lost in your work is neither a weakness nor a strength. It's a tendency, or perhaps a characteristic or a trait. It becomes a strength if you recognize when it's beneficial to allow yourself to forget the time. It becomes a weakness when you either can't discern that it doesn't always work, or deny it and disregard others when they share with you it's not working. When you know it doesn't work, yet do nothing effective to accommodate yourself with such a tendency, it becomes soul neglect.

Weaknesses don't necessarily need to be changed as much as they need to be expressed through a soul-fulfilling approach to work. This is possible when they are acknowledged and accommodated. Choosing to acknowledge and accommodate them is being on the path of purpose because you're improving *upon* them.

Ask yourself, "What can I give to myself to accommodate my weaknesses?"

When I notice an urge to analyze, judge, or push myself to make tough decisions, I use it as a signal to assess the appropriateness of those abilities and make a new choice if I deem fear and my ego have crept into the driver's seat. When that happens, I use the OPEN Method to give me a double, sometimes triple, dose of velocity for clarity, confidence, and conviction. It becomes a conscious choice to transform thoughts, urges, or feelings that don't serve me, or anyone else, into a maximum return of productive outcomes.

Recognizing this habit, I can forgive myself for times I indulged it when it didn't make sense to do so. For any new routine we take into our lives, we must develop muscle. Eventually, a muscle I developed over time was thanking myself for not just the tendency I had but for the ability to assess when to use it and when to move on, by nurturing myself first and then allowing a soul-fulfilling approach to surface naturally.

Get a Consistent Approach to Fitness

In addition to skill development, a fitness practice trains your brain to believe what you say and that your behavior matters—it's a great form of esteem development! A consistent weekly approach is a gift to your body, mind, and soul! Whether you Engage in fitness twice or five times a week doesn't matter. It's a regular, consistent approach that matters most. Find what works for you and be consistent.

Get Involved in Improving Workplace Issues

Another way to improve self-esteem is to get involved. At your job, you cannot complain about how things function, do nothing to try to fix them, and then expect your sense of personal power to improve. Doing nothing IS doing something. It is agreeing to stay stuck. No matter what your reasons are for your mindset and behavior, you are either actively contributing to things improving, staying the same, or getting worse, both at work and in your life.

Some of the most powerful initiatives to advocate for if you are feeling powerless at your job are these:

- **Advocate for resources**—advocate for whatever you and others require to do your jobs well. That means asking without being attached to a "yes" answer; the opposite is whining, bullying, or getting pushy. Being open to a "yes," a "no," or a counteroffer brings cooperative energy to the situation. A lack of resources alone can contribute to feelings of powerlessness. Advocating for them can help to maintain your personal power whether or not you receive what you request.

- **Build relationships**—as we learned with nurturing civility, support and encouragement matter big time! It's easier to get these from people if they know, like, and trust you, so get involved in things where you get to know, like, and trust others too! Studies show that people who feel supported at work report feeling more engaged and enjoy a greater sense of well-being and accomplishment than people who don't enjoy supportive relationships at work.[23] Remember, *support* does not mean having a buddy you complain with or share quips with about how you feel powerless. Support comes from relationships that move you toward clarity, confidence, and conviction.

- **Understand goals**—the more you can see how your work directly impacts the organization you work for, its goals, and the people it serves, the more likely you will feel as though your contribution matters.

Additional Strategies to Build Personal Power

Here are a few extra ideas on building your esteem, confidence, and power. These ideas focus on setting yourself up to experience accomplishment being alive and well in your life and in giving yourself what you may not be getting from your job at this time. Try any one of these that appeals to you:

- **Set and accomplish "fifty-feet-farther-ahead goals".** When I am overwhelmed or depleted, I think about two things I can do to get myself fifty feet farther ahead in my day. Only when these two things are done do I think of two more things. Try this focused approach to your day.

- **Reward yourself.** If you are experiencing a lack of rewards on the job, it's time to treat yourself. Reward yourself for small accomplishments such as decluttering an area of your office or home, signing up for an esteem-development class, finishing a self-help book.

- **Declutter.** To get a power surge, give yourself a clutter purge! Get rid of what no longer serves you. Clean out your workspace in the office and clean out your house. Start with one room, closet, cabinet, drawer, or area of the garage or basement. If you haven't used it in the past year, or it's not in good working order, that's a good sign it might be time to let it go or replace it. Marie Kondo is an expert in this area. Check out her books and TV shows *Tidying Up with Marie Kondo* and *Sparking Joy with Marie Kondo*.

- **Change up your routine.** Here are a few ideas: drive a different route to work, sit in a different seat when taking public transportation, try a new breakfast routine or flavor of coffee, stand at your desk versus sitting all day. The point here is to disrupt your stagnant efforts by injecting new scenery and perspectives into your brain. Deliberate action in this safe and easy way can remind you that you have new choices available to you all the time. You also have the power to take advantage of them.

- **Affirmations.** Learn about the power of affirmations. Louise Hay is the pioneer in this area. You can check out her books online. You can also do a search on *How can I learn about affirmations?* on google and a lot of resources will show up for you to read through. Affirmations are a powerful way to rewire our brain to think with more strength for what is wanted versus unwanted.

- **Say "thank you".** The simple act of saying thank you (and nothing more) trains your brain that you don't have to explain, justify, share, respond to, or counteroffer everything. Simply say "thank you" when offered a compliment, help, or favor. As the OPEN

Method asks you to just be with your thoughts, urges, and feelings, the thank-you strategy is asking you just to receive and be with another's generosity and your worthiness. The important step here is learning to "zip it" after you say "thank you".

- **Learn something new** you always wanted to try. This is a great way to nurture yourself. It's never too late to indulge an old interest or explore a new one.

When It's Time to Quit

We all have moments when we fantasize about quitting our jobs. But when the occasional fantasy becomes a chronic feeling, we become transformed into a credentialed expert at noticing more and more evidence that our job or workplace is a drain. When that happens, it pushes us closer to the brink of quitting on the spot.

Is that you? Are you an expert at noticing evidence that your job or place of work is a drain? How advanced are you in this? Which of these statements most closely resembles what you'd say about your desire to quit?

1. "That's it! I'm outta here!"
2. "F*ck this place!"
3. "F*ck you, you f*ck'n F*CK!" (the "you" here may refer to the boss, the customers, your co-workers, the work environment, the job itself or any/all of the above).

If you picked the first statement, you might be at risk for noticing more and more offenses that seem to be pushing you to the brink of signing a resignation letter.

If you picked the second, you might not be quite ready to sign a resignation letter and throw it at your boss (not without another job lined up), but you probably have your resume out there. You might also be scaring someone you love—they may think any day from now you will light up a cigar and pour a celebratory drink because you quit on the spot even though you don't have another job lined up.

If you picked the third, however—MEDIC!! It's imperative you get yourself some healing—stat! Your view of the situation may be so damaged that you can't make a clear and confident decision about what to do on your own. In the process of such feelings festering for too long, you're no doubt causing harm to others—those who probably deserve it—but to innocent bystanders as well.

Maybe your urge to quit is tame and refined right now, occurring to you as a cerebral, dignified, brilliant idea. It might have you saying something like "Perhaps it's time I start looking for another job—one more fitting and worthy of my impeccable knowledge, skills, and abilities."

Are you feeling ready to quit? The truth is you can recover and heal from the daily effects of your job especially if you are going through a tough time that you know will soon pass.

But what if you are not so sure this tough time at your job is a passing phase? Do you have this unsettled feeling about your job? Are the demanding conditions an expected way of life—and it's not what you want for your life? Is your fight, flight, or freeze instinct kicking in? Are you wanting to run (quietly and quickly) or stirring up a heap of trouble due to feeling backed into that same corner where all the other "misunderstood and undervalued" employees are hanging out? Are you fighting with some poor souls who might deserve it—and even some who don't? Maybe the time has come to make a drastic move right out the company front door. Here's how to know.

Emotional Wealth Building

There are a few components to get clear about when you're deciding if it makes sense to just quit your job without another means of income or employment. The first thing to do is to practice building emotional wealth.

Emotional wealth building is about actively building your emotional stamina so that you can cope with your work situation as it is now. This is a time to nurture yourself—big time! You need a clear head to figure out your next move and to know what will nurture you until you get to the dream job, hit the lottery, or retire. You also need the stamina to be able to see how you will be bigger, better, faster, stronger as a result of the experience that has you wanting to quit.

Decide right now (write it out), what you will do every day to give yourself a break or time to recover from the current troubles of your job. It's important that you write out this plan with the strategies you will try as outlined in this book because there is no one remedial plan that works for everyone. I suggest you look at areas of your job and/or personal life that are draining you and decide one strategy for each area (relationship with the boss, relationship with other people at work, lack of resources, projects, home, childcare issues, etc.). Ask yourself, "What will I do daily to heal, recover, and build my emotional wealth from the areas of work and life that I want to quit?"

Choices that Will Not Help

I encourage you to make these choices:

- Do NOT talk about your job to anyone who can't directly help you address anything. Don't complain about your job while spending time with your friends and don't talk about their job troubles either.

- Do NOT hang out with people where there is a lack of reciprocity in the relationship. Some people might be hard to avoid so if you can't avoid them have a plan to recoup from your time with them.

- Do NOT self-medicate. It's one thing to enjoy your favorite drinks once in a while, it's another thing to overindulge everyday.

- Do NOT zone out on video games every night. More than one hour of video game playing a day lowers your consciousness.

- Do NOT force or push yourself to figure things out or perform work when you are depleted. It's never a good idea to create anything with depleted, cynical, or powerless energy. It often guarantees unproductive or unsustainable results.

- Do NOT continue in the job with no plan for how to cope with continued exposure to a situation that draws from your too low emotional bank account.

Daily emotional wealth building enables you to become capable of making an informed decision about whether or not it makes sense to just quit without having another job or means of income. Not Engaging in an active plan to recover is like making daily purchases on your debit or credit card but never adding any money into your accounts. Eventually the bank will shut you down and you will risk bankruptcy and maybe even exposure as being fraudulent in your practices. The effects of draining job demands are cumulative. It's a debt that racks up and eventually it manifests as health issues if left unaddressed. In my experience, emotional debt at work is a fast track to actual financial debt depending how quickly you can heal, how much you have in your financial accounts to draw from, and if you have other means of income.

Deciding on the Next Move

There are three factors that matter greatly for deciding whether you should stay or go, even without another job lined up:

1. What are the problems you are facing at work? Values conflicts are the most important consideration. List out the problems that are contributing to you feeling like you want to quit. Then list any values you have that each problem is in conflict with.

2. Do you have mostly high or low control over the situation you are facing at work? Once you list out the problems you observe as reasons to quit, assign a number for how much control you have over each problem. Score your control level using this system: 0 for none, 1 for low, 2 for some, and 3 for ample.

3. How easy is it for you to think your thoughts, feel your urges and feelings, and nurture yourself so that more productive responses can surface? Assign a number for how much is left in your "emotional bank account" to respond productively to that problem using the same scoring system.

Problem	Value(s)	Control (0-3)	Response (0-3)

If you believe you have low emotional control and low problem control over problems that violate values you hold—do two things ASAP:

1. Get some time off from your job if you can. This is one of the most effective times to use your sick or vacation days.

2. Seek help from a career coach or a therapist plus a doctor if you are already experiencing physical symptoms.

Get in touch with someone who is qualified to help you sort through your unique situation and help you build confidence for what to do next. Sometimes it does make sense to quit and move on. Especially if your health and/or emotional well-being is at stake. A good career coach can help you do this: figure out your next move; get a life plan for how to handle the impacts of leaving your job; and guide you on how to explain this transition to future employers.

If you have any thoughts at all about quitting your job, you are living in agreement that there's something wrong with your current job, employer, or work environment. This erroneously identifies the problem as being outside of yourself, leaving you powerless and in victim mode. In identifying the problem as being external, you put yourself in a situation that is likely to build velocity for revealing more and more false evidence that justifies emotional quitting AND for setting yourself up for a similar situation in your next job.

The truth is the two of you together may very well be a mismatch that is producing mutual collateral damage. Feeling you want to quit your job may be a signal that you are just ready to expand on doing "your work"? In other words, are you "running away from" something or "running toward" something greater?

If you are ready to quit and want to be transitioned to a job you love much faster and more easily, assess which list is longer—what you are "running toward" or what you are "running away from." A longer list of "running toward" something is a signal that the soul is in control and ready to expand. A longer list of "running away from" something is a signal that the ego is in control and that you are in victim mode. Nurturing a thought that you are a victim restricts you to three reactive options—fight, flight or freeze. Are you ready to bail (flight reaction)? Or are you fighting with people at your job (fight reaction)? Or are you unsure what to do and feeling stuck at your job (freeze reaction)?

If just don't like the job, work environment, work conditions, or boss, you will be in pain. But if you feel powerless to prove your value in it, you will suffer. Being in pain or suffering diminishes your ability to be clear if your best option is ...

1. to stay and face the problem—which is really an opportunity to overcome some chronic fear or recurring personal challenge

   or

2. to realize that you have outgrown the job. This is usually the case if you used to enjoy the job and then things seem to inexplicably change. Do you wonder why you no longer feel so warm and fuzzy about the job, place, boss, or tasks?

The real problem may be that you have something to contribute, which you may not be fully in touch with just yet. You can't offer what's not clear to you or what you don't believe is possible to offer or would be valued if it were offered. Could the job be presenting a situation that provides an opportunity for you to overcome or discover something personal or innate within you? Maybe you are to discover what you truly have to offer and wish to be valued for. If you don't "face the beast" at this job, I assure you it will show up at the next job. The universe never lets us off the hook for our development. If you don't face it in your current job, you will only recognize job opportunities that present the same problems over and over again.

Or is it just time to go—time to spread your wings further and grow somewhere else that needs you more?

When we have outgrown a job or work environment and yet we stay, it keeps us contracted and feeling restricted. What would it feel like to wear shoes all day, every day that were too small, too narrow, too wide, too not your style, too unsupportive for your preferred comfort, too wrong for the weather? You'd probably be in pain, be crabby, complain about the shoes a lot, and be dying to get home to get those shoes off and into a pair that felt perfect. Right? No doubt you and this job are a poor fit right now on some level. But that doesn't necessarily make the job, work environment, or boss bad, wrong and terrible. It's probably a perfect fit for "someone else's feet."

Do you believe you have something to offer that your current job would not value? Here's the secret for being ushered more quickly and painlessly toward another opportunity that will be a better fit and value you more—offer it anyway while you craft your exit plan!!

As an HR executive and career coach, I have never seen anyone get into unforgivable trouble by contributing anything that is offered with an intention of bringing value to others. In my experience, people who do that (even if they make a mistake) are called "valued employees"—not "perfect employees." How we offer value to others is unique to each of us—it is "your work." Your job is the means by which you offer "your work." Your work is more than the tasks you are responsible for. Being focused on just the tasks required by your job is like making food without putting any love into it. We all have tasted the difference in food made with love versus food made by someone who just doesn't want to cook. Yum versus yuck! Bland at best.

Offering what you have to offer without regard for whether or not it is deserved may be the surest route to building your sense of power and confidence. Plus, you might be surprised at how "your work" is received. Even if it isn't received the way you want it to be, it doesn't matter. You will be operating in agreement that you have valuable contributions to make that can make a difference for others. If your current job truly doesn't value that (or deserve it), you will be ushered more quickly and painlessly toward another opportunity that will.

Resolving issues that have you feeling like your job is not a good fit with your values, life ambitions, or the resources you believe you require to perform your job effectively is the predictor of either restoring engagement or evolving further toward burnout within one year.[24] The world needs you to restore your engagement, grow, and evolve.

You deserve to contribute in a place that truly values what you have to offer and gives you what you require to contribute authentically and fully. The energy of the universe will respond to your engaged energy. It will usher you to that place more quickly and painlessly when you make a habit of nurturing yourself and restoring your capacity for energy, civility, and power.

CHAPTER 12

STEP 4—NURTURE FOR THE N IN OPEN

An empty lantern provides no light. Self-care is the fuel that allows your light to shine brightly.

Unknown

Give to Yourself

To Nurture is to give care to, or to encourage the growth, development, or restoration of someone or something, *especially to yourself in times of burnout.* Nurturing is giving yourself what you decided would help you feel better in the Engage phase. In step 4 of the OPEN Method, you get into action. You give to yourself without guilt or self-judgment so you can experience being cared for, calmly and securely, as you face your challenges, and restore your senses of power, purpose, and peace. This act of kindness directed inward welcomes the development of productive thoughts, urges, and feelings that lead to engagement for your work and life to surface on their own. The primary aspect of Nurturing is soul-fulfilling self-care. The secondary aspect is accepting support from others.

Two things might be challenging in this step:

1. Deciding to give to yourself what you identified in Step 3—Engage.
2. Giving it to yourself without guilt or judgement.

I know you may think it could be risky to advocate for some of the strategies to heal exhaustion, cynicism, and powerlessness. What if your employer, family, or peers judge you harshly? What might it mean about you if you took time to heal yourself?

Don't think of it as risky or selfish. Think of deciding to try any of these strategies as an investment in yourself. For all the years you attended school, an investment was made in your learning (tuition, books, supplies, clothing, transportation, meals, participating in class trips, clubs, and activities). This investment may have been the primary responsibility of your parents or guardians, or maybe yourself. Investment in learning and personal growth does not go away after graduation. Rather, it stays with you throughout your life; you are now the primary party responsible for the investment.

Advocating for or investing in what you require is an opportunity to restore your sense of personal power and get back to making a meaningful difference for yourself and others. No amount of money is too much to increase your own sense of worth. Plus, don't expect anyone, including your employer, to pay for something you are not willing to pay for. You wouldn't deny yourself healthcare if you needed it, would you? Personal growth that prevents burnout could be the greatest investment you make for your own health!

Remember, engaging in any of the remedial strategies that resonated with you does not mean getting what you want from others. Your power to restore yourself to engagement and open up a path to a sense of purpose comes from deliberately enabling and protecting your well-being. Approaching your well-being with that kind of energy breeds vigor, civility, and personal power. It also raises your ability to be engaged at your job, and persevere on the path of power, purpose, and peace for your work and your life.

The Power of Decision

Nurturing's best friend is decision. How interesting that other words for *decision* include *conclusion, determination,* and *call.* They are synonymous! A decision IS a *conclusion* (already having what you want). A decision IS a *determination* that leads to persistence. A decision IS a "call" or a "calling." It's an action that brings meaning into our lives. When we decide to execute any of the strategies that appealed to us in step 3, we are just at the beginning of a process that requires *persistence* toward a more and more vivid experience of feeling cared for by ourselves. This feeling of care enables us to be able to care for others in ways that are meaningful. Caring for others allows a sense of engagement and fulfillment from our work and lives in return. A decision to walk the path of purpose is a commitment to give your attention and energy to what will expand your ability to experience a sense of engagement and receive a sense of fulfillment.

Practicing the first three steps of the OPEN Method is not enough. When we make *decisions* to act on what we identified in step 3, we actually have it as long as we continue to follow through on our decision. That means doing things that enable us to experience the unfolding of our decision. It also means saying *no* to things that sabotage the possibility of our decision becoming a more vivid reality.

We also don't have Nurturing just by *envisioning it.* Many of us blame the experience of indecision on a lack of vision (we can't figure out what we want). But the truth is there is probably

> We may not always know what we want, but we always know what we don't want.

a hesitation with owning our vision once we create it versus actually not being able to figure out what we want in the first place. We may not always know what we want, but we always know what we don't want.

As we learned, we can take any thought such as "What I don't want is … " and imagine an opposite state. So could the real blame be with the decision to actually have and be accountable for creating what we want?

Part of manifesting engagement for your work, and being able to connect to a sense of purpose, is being kind and loving to yourself. Nurturing acts toward yourself when you feel drained, depleted, stuck, or challenged keep you grounded in an energy that will facilitate you in being reengaged with your work, life, and other people.

Experiences that drain, deplete, or perplex you aren't a problem. Doing nothing to restore and keep your energy full *is* a problem.

If you are still allowing your attention, time, effort, energy, and what you talk about to be things that don't open your ability to be engaged, connected to power, purpose, and peace for your work and your life, then you are not in the Nurturing stage. You are still in the Observe stage. If so, no worry. Simply go back to step 1 and proceed from there once more. No guilt, no judgment.

No Guilt and No Judgment

Let me say that three times so it sinks in:

> Give yourself what you require without guilt or judgment.
>
> Give Yourself What You Require without Guilt OR Judgment.
>
> Give Yourself What You Require WITHOUT GUILT OR JUDGMENT!

Listen, it's okay to notice and experience guilt or self-judgment. It might be your reason for feeling stuck, less than engaged, or burned out. However, it's not okay to let such feelings be excuses for why you don't Nurture yourself so that you can heal from trauma or disengagement.

Would you judge a tired, overwhelmed child for needing a nap, a hug, a shoulder to cry on, a favorite *blankie* or toy? I hope not. When you are depleted, your ego (your inner child) has worked itself into a state of overextension, disengagement and/or ineffectiveness. Like kids who nap daily or have a favorite toy for comfort, adults also need a regular flow of something to restore their depleted energy. Unlike the way it is for kids, our signals that we need to restore aren't always as clear. Could that be because as we get older we deny our need for restorative comforts as a way to demonstrate our responsibleness, strength, maturity, virility, and so on. Actually, it doesn't seem very strong or responsible at all to shut out, ignore, deny, or disconnect from our well-being. It actually seems quite weak and reckless to me. Would you agree? Reading your depleted signals and taking action to restore yourself might require an act of courage from you.

If you feel compelled to know why you might judge Nurturing as a weakness or why you might experience guilt for having moments of emotional discomfort, take a look at your family of origin. Did you receive messages at an early age that reinforce your current beliefs or feelings?

I once had a client share with me that he was taught at an early age "If your success wasn't hard, it doesn't count as success." I shared with him I may not be a good coach for him if he wasn't ready to honor that nugget of guidance from his parents for what it was intended to do for him as a child and surrender as an adult to a more sustainable way of achieving fulfillment and success. I was direct, explaining I do not condone success at the expense of anyone's well-being or wellness. He got it. He realized that was a belief that had landed him in burn-out at too young an age, and he was now open to a more sustainable approach. I admired the courage it took for him to acknowledge that and get onto the path of purpose.

Perhaps a professional psychotherapist can help you to accept guilt more comfortably as part of your process. I am a strong advocate of professional psychotherapy to accompany you in your pivot-to-purpose journey. Guilt or self-judgment taught in early life was probably offered to you out of some form of protection and care for your ability to be a moral, functioning adult. Experiencing guilt or self-judgment as an adult may require you to approach your return to engagement as an act of courage. Over time, the guilt you feel will be more bearable. The bullying voice inside that shames you for being "weak" will morph in time into more like a whispered thought from your past. You will notice this sentiment from your ego yet it will no longer have the power it once had to stop you from doing what connects you with purpose. Experiences of guilt or harsh self-judgment are merely part of the process of learning to practice the OPEN Method. They will naturally move your ego from the driver's seat, to the passenger's seat, to the backseat, before eventually settling into a child's car seat where they will be neatly secure, tucked in, adorable, and harmless while your soul drives and regularly practices the OPEN Method.

Anytime you are irritated at another person or a situation you are in, it's a sign you need to do something Nurturing for yourself. Why? Because when you are depleted, you can only see problems and their resolution as being outside yourself. That will drive and falsely justify you in doing and saying things that will probably only make the situation worse. They will keep what you want farther out of reach. Desperate people do (and say) desperate things. Often, nothing makes us feel more desperate than when we believe control is in another's hands, especially if we don't trust that person to do what we believe is the right thing.

Things we say to ourselves or aloud to people who have nothing to do with our grievances are only ways of not looking at ourselves, our hopes, our fears, our power, or our limitations. We fear that if we looked at ourselves, we might judge ourselves as inadequate.

You'll know if you are in a self-limiting state of being if your view of yourself, your life, your situation, or another is stressed or fear-based. These limiting states might be evidenced by judgment-filled or guilt-ridden thoughts, urges, and feelings. Guilt and harsh self-judgment are useful signals for letting you know it's time to practice the OPEN

Method. Your inner dialogue could be what lets you know when it's time to do so, because you'll say fear-based, egocentric things like one of these examples:

- **aggravation**—"Extra demands and stress! Great! Just what I need!"

- **self-judgment**—"No one else took a vacation this year. I don't think it would be right if I went away."

- **judgment of others**—"No matter what I do, it's just not enough for this person! (INSERT NAME) is just a jerk!"

- **incorrigibility**—"This place sucks. It will never change. I just wanna quit."

- **defensiveness**—"No good deed goes unpunished! Next time, I'll just keep my mouth shut."

- **lack of empathy**—"I just don't understand people! How could they think such thoughts? There must be something wrong with them."

- **denial**—"I'm fine. I'll get through it."

- **offensiveness**—"Everyone is so pissy and whiny. Just shut the f*** up and let's do what we gotta do, people!"

- **vengefulness**—"I'm tired of being overlooked! I'll show them just how much they would suffer without me around!"

Saying things to yourself like the phrases above puts the power of resolve outside yourself while welcoming states such as anger, resentment, complaint, blame, or defeat, all of which block engagement. As Brené Brown, research professor at the University of Houston and author of several #1 *New York Times* bestsellers, reminds us of this through the title of a journal she wrote, "*Talk to yourself like you would to someone you love.*" Brené Brown famously writes that the most compassionate people have boundaries for how they will allow others to treat them and how they talk to themselves.

Limiting states happen to everyone. When they happen, people seldom infer it would be wise to just go do some self-Nurturing work for a while. We can no longer tolerate pushing forward without giving ourselves something to restore what has been depleted. Staying in action with depleted energy fosters solutions and connections born from depleted thoughts, urges, and feelings. That is birthing into the world what is sure to be unstable and ineffective. When we birth ideas and service from depleted energy, we subconsciously send out a vibe to the world that we would like that same energy offered back to us. So, if we direct depleted energy such as guilt at ourselves or others, we are only enabling guilt-inducing treatment from others onto ourselves. Depleted energy cannot discern what it has to offer, nor can it stop automatically answering blind calls for help. It's a learned skill to answer cries for help with service that includes honoring boundaries and taking time to restore when depleted. It's an even greater learned skill to know and accept that you may have nothing to offer other than love and acceptance from a distance.

We must let go of our guilt or judgment for practicing the OPEN Method. It's not enough to Observe, Pause, and Engage. We must actually do it with love too. How do you feel when someone offers you their listening through a filter of "Fine, I'll listen to you, but know you're bothering me!" Or keeps shutting down what you are sharing by bringing the conversation back, over and over, to "What about me?" Or when you get an insincere apology that includes a "sor-ray" spoken through an eye roll, folded arms, and judgment that you're being too sensitive? I'm sure you don't like it. Nor does it suffice or draw you closer to that person. Yet you can't control or change it if that's what you get. People only offer what's easily available to them to offer. Thankfully, what will really help you isn't outside yourself anyway. Restoring your energy starts with Nurturing yourself.

Everything we think, do, and say is an affirmation. We cast spells like a sorcerer who only has power to bring the words they utter about another onto themself. The power you have over others is the power they allow you to have. So in fact, you have no real power over others. You do, however, have total power over yourself.

> Everything we think, do, and say is an affirmation. We cast spells like a sorcerer who only has power to bring the words they utter about another onto themself.

We all go through dark times especially with our jobs. What's even more scary than facing dark times is not giving yourself fuel to face them or time to restore from them.

Receiving Nurturing Support from Others

I mentioned that Nurturing from others is secondary to the Nurturing you give yourself. The best Nurturing we can get from others comes when we share what we are going through and ask for their support. Sometimes it also includes telling another person what support actually looks like for you. Support does not mean finding someone you can complain to about events that upset you. Don't make talking about what happened that upset you the main point. Doing so just makes you relive events that triggered your thoughts, urges, and feelings in the first place; this could be soul abusive. Instead, be sure to include dialogue about how you feel about your relationships or the situation that contributed to your upset. Add what you want your relationships or situation to be.

If you must vent, don't give more air time to what happened than you do to talking about the solution you desire. Confide in people who offer support, or perhaps coaching, with a goal of getting in communication with the people you may need to restore balance with. If there are people you are ready to mend fences with, learning effective communication strategies might help. I named one of my favorites in chapter 10—Nonviolent Communication. A simple thing I learned from someone who received Nonviolent Communication training is to use the phrase "Would you be willing to (*insert your request here*)" when asking for help or negotiating toward resolution with others. For example, "Would you be willing to listen to me about a problem I am facing at work and offer me your ideas about how to achieve the outcome I'd like to achieve?"

The Key to Successful Nurturing

Nurturing, whether from yourself or others, is loving. It often comes from a place of believing that your situation will either get better or indeed never change. Either way, you will certainly be wiser and stronger for having had the experience. Nurturing isn't eating a pint of ice cream while asking yourself, "What's the use?" Nor is it declaring "Nothing will ever get better" while you wait for some imagined fate that's worse than death. Time spent in the OPEN Method is evidence that we are in the process of moving toward wiser and stronger engagement for our work and life. A wiser, stronger, win-win solution is only possible if we choose to surface wiser, stronger, win-win solutions.

The second you decide you want wiser, stronger, win-win solutions to surface and you keep practicing the OPEN Method, what follows is the perfect unfolding of your ability to notice and participate joyfully in wiser, stronger, win-win experiences. In addition, you will be better prepared to responsibly handle the internal and material consequences of that choice. The Nurturing step requires that you shift your focus from how things will play out to gaining clarity for your choices and taking care of yourself while life aligns itself to answer you. Surrendering how the alignment will happen enables your soul and ego to work together and notice opportunities offering a sense of engagement and purpose for your work and life. Stop putting yourself on the hook for *how* and start putting yourself on the hook for noticing and participating in opportunities that will bring you in closer alignment with *what* you want.

As Step 4 requires you to say, "Yes!" to what you want, it also requires you to say, "No!" to what you don't want. Saying "No" is often harder than getting clear about what we want. The truth is when we see things happen that seem counter to what we want, we use it as evidence that what we want won't happen or that we had no right to want it in the first place.

This is not evidence.

Instead, it's just an opportunity to say, "No, thanks." Simply saying, "No" versus making something mean we can't have what we want reinforces that we're serious about what we want. It makes anything contrary to what we want not okay.

When stuff doesn't go your way, are you inclined to question or doubt yourself? Questioning, doubting, or wanting things to happen more quickly than they are happening are all forms of resistance. Shift your view from resistance to instead see the opportunity to say, "No, thank you." This reinforces your connection with what you want. There is no need to settle. It's okay to notice every doubtful thought coming into your head. When that happens, tell your protective ego, "Thanks for the thought and I'm going to go with what I decided to experience more vividly anyway."

Doubtful thoughts from the ego are like employees who work in your head and believe their job is to protect you. They see all new thoughts, approaches, and ideas as threats.

> Doubtful thoughts from the ego are like employees who work in your head and believe their job is to protect you.

When you're feeling drained—follow the OPEN Method:

> Step 1—**Observe** what you think, have an urge to do or say, and feel.
>
> Step 2—**Pause** to be with what you think, have an urge to do or say, and feel. Pause until you are ready to decide when you will Engage in figuring out what would feel Nurturing.
>
> Step 3—**Engage** by actively deciding what you will do to Nurture yourself.

Step 4—**Nurture** yourself. Do it! Give yourself what you decided would be Nurturing from the Engage phase.

It's time to retain your power and ability to connect to a sense of purpose and experience engagement for your work, your life, and yourself. You can start your journey toward purpose by recognizing fear or stress as a call for practicing the OPEN Method without guilt or judgment. This way courageous action that serves everyone can surface.

CHAPTER 13

THE OPEN METHOD IN ACTION

Applying the OPEN Method

Exhaustion can start as subtly as not wanting to get out of bed to go to work. Now we all experience that feeling from time to time but when it happens more often than not, it can be an indicator that you might be on the path to burnout. So, let's apply the OPEN Method to the situation of not wanting to get out of bed to go to work.

This is a simple example demonstrating a way to align with energy, civility, and personal power instead of seeking support from ineffective sources. You don't need to rely on excessive amounts of caffeine, a countdown to lunch, or even the weekend to cope with facing your day. Such reliances only equip you to recognize unsustainable sources of comfort for the wounds inflicted by the job you may feel powerless to change.

Step 1—Observe

After the alarm goes off, what are the first thoughts, urges, and feelings you experience when you wake up in the morning to go to work?

Notice your thoughts. Are they something like one of these?

- "Oy, I shouldn't have had that much beer before bed last night."
- "What day is it? Oh crap! It's Wednesday. I want it to be Friday!"
- "Is it 6:00 a.m. already? But I'm so damn tired!"
- "Only eighty-two more days until my vacation! I can't wait!"
- "At least this job isn't as bad as my last job. I hate that I have to work at all."
- "Thank God, I have a job. But why do I stay when I'm not happy?"

Notice your urges. Are they something like one of these?

- An urge to hit the snooze button
- An urge to call in sick
- An urge to roll over and readjust your position—snuggle in tighter!

Notice your feelings. Are they something like one of these?

- Sad: disappointed it's morning already?
- Angry or aggravated: upset you didn't sleep well?
- Cynical: anticipating a bad day?
- Depressed: crushed to face another day on the job?
- Afraid: stressed about the presentation you have to give to the board today?

> Because we don't have our wits about us when we first wake up, our first thoughts are often very authentic.

Louise Hay taught us that the words we speak (in our head and out loud) reveal our thought patterns. Because we don't have our wits about us when we first wake up, our first thoughts are often very authentic. If your first thought on waking up holds more love for your bed than it does for your job—yet you want a job you love—then know you are the one sabotaging your ability to experience love for a job. When the words we speak don't match the hopes we hold with the actions we take, we are deceiving ourselves. We are unaware that we have not yet built our capacity to joyfully have what we want.

How does what you think, want to do, say to yourself, or feel about not wanting to get out of bed to go to work make you feel? Allow those answers to come up and be with them. Maybe you're not in touch with what you think, want to do, say to yourself, or feel. Could it be that you're avoiding connecting with the thoughts, urges, and feelings you hold about your job?

If each morning presents initial thoughts, urges, and feelings about your job that are more aligned with burnout than engagement, that's okay. Don't judge yourself, but don't settle either. Don't settle for adverse or unclear thoughts to be in your head when you take your first action of the day, even if that action is just heading for the bathroom. Flush the fear-based or fuzzy thoughts along with the rest of your waste down the toilet! You don't deserve a day that doesn't excite you or that drains you without promise of recovery. Allowing adverse or unclear thoughts, urges, and feelings about your day to perpetuate is only aligning yourself with situations that will reinforce that you deserve more disengaging experiences. So acknowledge your thoughts, urges, and feelings, but then train yourself to let them guide you to opposite thoughts, urges, and feelings about what you want to experience.

There's no need to journal or write anything down in the Observe phase. Simply notice and own that you have thoughts, urges, and feelings that sabotage engagement. Notice that when they are allowed to perpetuate, they create a web that keeps you stuck exactly where you are but probably don't want to be.

Your less-than-engaged state may be evidenced by using words that describe what you don't want versus what you do want. Remember this from chapter 10:

- *don't, won't, can't, should, shouldn't, have to* versus *will*
- *but* versus *and*
- *without, not* versus *with*
- *need* versus *require*
- *want* versus *have*

Are your thoughts focused on stuff you don't wanna do? If so, you are in a less-than-engaged state and it's time to move to the next step. And the next step is to Pause.

Step 2—Pause

Since this example is about going to work, you probably won't give yourself much time to Pause if you choose not to be late. Here is a brief example of Pause that can be powerful if you truly are mindful of being with your observations.

How does it feel to be with the thoughts you have about not wanting to go to work? What urges are you resisting? How does it feel to feel what you feel about not wanting to go to work? Does the support of your pillow around your head and neck, the texture of sheets and blankets, your dreamy thoughts, or the warmth coming from your pet or partner make you want to stay in bed? Are the minor comforts offered by your bed a greater possibility for experiencing engagement for your work and life than seeing what *could* happen in your day?

How do those thoughts, urges, and feelings make you feel?

Just be with any resistance, negotiations, or counteroffers created by your ego. Acknowledge your ego for how clever it is. Decide how long you will be with your observed thoughts, urges, and feelings. Maybe it's five more seconds, five more minutes, or longer, but, hopefully, not so long that it will create more stress than necessary.

Step 3—Engage

The next step is to Engage.

Perhaps while you are still in bed you begin to identify solutions that could give yourself meaningful care. Care is giving yourself loving service that you would be happy and even excited to receive, no matter how small the gesture. If it's a gesture that comes from an intention of restoring your depleted state, it counts. The purpose of engaging with the idea of these gestures is to enable yourself to naturally emerge solutions and actions.

Remember, in Step 3—Engage, I offer you lots of strategies for nurturing your vigor, civility, and power, and I encourage you to try them one at a time. So, for this example, let's look at engaging in soul-fulfillment in the context of not wanting to get out of bed to go to work from the perspective of creating a *values experience*. Ask yourself this: *Which of the things in this short list do I most value and enjoy experiencing?* Pick as many as you like, or make up your own things—but focus on only one to start with.

abundance

accomplishment

adventure

beauty

creativity

family

friendship

fun

helping others

learning

social activity

wellness

This is your value word. So, whether you sit on the edge of your bed feeling around for your fuzzy slippers, or lie there taking a moment to wipe the sleep from your eyes, this is probably the same moment you start asking yourself, "How can I experience my value word?"

Let's say you choose *beauty*.

If a few depleting thoughts about the day are still creeping in, simply say: "Wait, erase that." Instead say this: "I'm so grateful for all the *beauty* I will get to experience today. I can't wait to see how *beauty* will prevail, even though I have a *full, busy and challenging day ahead of me.*" Let the "even though I have" statement be the thing you fear or stress about experiencing.

Next, decide a strategy that will get you fifty-feet-farther-ahead in experiencing your value word of *beauty*. You might say something like this to yourself: "To start this day of *beauty*, I will give myself my favorite smelling body gel and candle light while I bathe in my bathroom." Decide what will make getting up easier or more enjoyable. Is it a body gel or lotion you love? Will it be a cozy robe you get to wear after your shower? Your favorite coffee? Think fifty-feet-farther-ahead versus jumping to lunch or 5:00 p.m., which is too far into the future of your day.

After the shower, determine the next two things you will do to enable *beauty*. Don't think beyond two things as it just gets too far into the future. Even if no specific ideas come about how you will experience your value word, your soul and ego will live your day on the lookout for things that will allow you to experience that value.

In each choice, decision, opportunity, question, offer, idea, or request that comes your way that day, take a moment to ask yourself, "Will it enable an experience of beauty?" Or "How can I bring the experience of beauty to this situation?"

Don't forget to also pat yourself on the back for engaging in meditation! A mere one to five minutes of solid focus on what you want to create is a form of meditation. So, here's a bonus hooray for you!

Step 4—Nurture

Next is to Nurture yourself. Go forward and give yourself what you decided to give yourself so that you can align yourself with well-being. Do it! Get up and get yourself that shower gel and light that candle. After your shower, give yourself more experiences of *beauty*? Think of two more fifty-feet-farther-ahead steps toward another experience of *beauty*. Remember, if you can't think of anything more, just move forward while staying conscious and alert for opportunities. These may come as ideas, suggestions from others, things you notice, what you hear or see others say or do that appeal to your decision to experience your value word. Go off on a treasure hunt for opportunities that will enable you to experience and participate in *beauty*, your value word.

What's most important is to note that you sabotage your ability to experience your value word if you instead stay focused on your anticipation of a day that is dreadfully full, busy, and challenging. Draining events will be much more faceable, tolerable, manageable, productive, and certainly recoverable if you take your value word with you throughout the day. Giving in to fear-based thoughts, urges, and feelings only enables you to notice and align with what makes you feel depleted and less than engaged versus nurtured and on the path of purpose. The choice to enjoy or dread your day, no matter what you may face, is yours.

CHAPTER 14

YOUR GREATEST OPPORTUNITY TO MAKE A MEANINGFUL DIFFERENCE

"Gnothi Seauton" (Know thyself)

Apollo

Stop Following Directions That Lead to the Path to Burnout

Over the course of my twenty year career as an HR executive, I have witnessed certain beliefs and behaviors that seem to eventually lead people into job burnout. What struck me most is that people do not realize that prolonged commitment to these beliefs and/or behaviors, without nurturing acts that enable them to heal and restore themselves, often sabotages their ability to sustain happiness through their work.

People innately know their value proposition (what they enable in the world), on a soul level, but may not always be able to recognize it or express it consciously. When we can't express something, it's as good as not having it at all. That leaves people vulnerable to believing their greatest opportunity for finding their path of purpose and success is to access it outside themselves. They tend to believe they have to find a winning team, get hired on to that winning team, and contribute by doing what is asked the way that others do it. This false sense of greatness can go all the way to the highest levels in an organization.

One of my executive clients once struggled in a new job. He began having candidate's remorse, asking himself, "What did I get myself into?" When we talked, I asked him what it was about the new culture or job that seemed to be misaligned with what he expected. He said, "I am used to working on winning teams. I thought this was a 'winning team.'"

Being surrounded only by people who also make, sell, and drink the same Kool-Aid you make, sell, and drink might feel as though you are in good company and that it's safe to do what you do. In fact it will probably also render you obsolete. If they already have and know how to make more Kool-Aid, why do they need you? Your greatest opportunity to make a meaningful difference is by offering what they don't already have or know. When you encounter others who seem to not have what you can offer, you will notice it as an opportunity versus a source of potential conflict. This happens naturally if you are on the path of purpose versus the path to burnout.

On the path of purpose, you magically forget about whether or not what you can offer is deserved. On this path, you only wish to alleviate others' pain through your talents, knowledge, skills, abilities, experience, and human nature. You wish to be of meaningful service. You no longer indulge an urge to look for evidence of whether or not your place of employment is worthy of your engagement.

As a former head of HR, I can assure you that it's a waste of time to wonder whether your current, past, or any future place of employment is worthy of your full engagement. In the context of work, whether what you offer is for someone's benefit or detriment doesn't matter. Surely no one *deserves* it. All beneficial work is an act of grace. What is worthy of your engagement is *you* PLUS *the individuals served by that organization* no matter how terrible their attitude or how undeservingly they may behave at times. Even though they may not *deserve* you, I assure you that they are *worthy* of your talents, knowledge, skills, abilities, experience, and human nature to be of meaningful service. In other words, even though their ego may be more appropriately met with retribution, punishment, or at least push-back, their soul is to be nurtured and honored for the virtuous possibilities it can enable in the world. How you treat others signals to the energy of the universe that you would welcome others treating you in the same manner.

The more you commit to offering your talents without regard for what you get in return, the faster you will be on a path to offering them where they will be appreciated and valued. Offering your talents regardless of what there is to get in return is what connects you with your power and a sustainable sense of fulfillment and purpose. Feeling appreciated and valued is a byproduct or a bonus gift. Mistakenly we think it's what makes us feel connected to our power and sustainable sense of fulfillment. We are also mistaken when we think that our greatest contribution is in getting others to receive what we are giving and in giving us whatever we hope for in return. There is no power or opportunity to sense fulfillment when we hold back on offering what we can do. We become vulnerable to holding back when we stop to consider whether or not our talents and abilities are deserved or if we fear being at risk of being misunderstood.

Your mind might come up with thoughts like these:

- "Well, they aren't very considerate of me. Why should I be of service to them?"
- "Last time I made a suggestion, they berated me in front of the entire team. Why should I put in any extra effort again?"

- "I'll just do what I am asked to do, even if I don't think it's the effective thing to do. Truthfully, I don't get paid for any more than that anyway!"

When you fall prey to a belief that what you can do matters only if others like it and will reward you in some way for it, you will feel justified in suppressing the talents and abilities embedded in your soul. You will elevate the false promises of protection offered by your ego. Eventually your sense of personal clarity, your connection with purpose, and your ability to engage in your work and enjoy it will suffer. Typically, we want others to take what we give (good or bad) with a spirit of "Thank God for you! You have enlightened me and now I can go onward, making the world a much better place because of your knowledge, ideas, gifts, kind gestures, and willingness to set me straight. Thank you for telling me what to do when I couldn't figure it out. Thank you for calling me out on being an ass when I mistakenly thought you were the problem. Thank you for helping me see all that you could do if only I gave you the opportunity, power, promotion, blah, blah, blah, etc., etc...."

Being focused on what others should and could do for you and allowing that to dictate what you will do for them in return aligns you with a sense of powerlessness. Eventually it also becomes exhausting and probably would leave the sweetest soul cynical. Why? Because you are merely reacting to others around you, thereby giving them all the power and control over you. Any whiff of risk that your contributions will be judged harshly or denied makes you feel justified in holding back. In return, holding back gets you a more and more vivid experience of feeling stuck, that the only good work is "hard" work, and that feeling content to be disconnected from a sense of purpose is okay as long as you make enough money.

In essence, I just shared with you directions to the path to burnout.

The Path to Burnout is More Likely With This Approach

The Path of Purpose is More Likely With This Approach

Start Offering What You Have to Offer, Even if You Get Fired for It

When we neglect nurturing ourselves when we feel drained, we will project onto our jobs, work environments, and others around us anything that is actually going on within us. We block our ability for self-clarity and our capacity to take care of ourselves in draining circumstances. So when we don't trust ourselves to take care of ourselves (maybe because we don't know how to), we will naturally perceive many people and situations as untrustworthy. Our ego slips into the driver's seat and causes us to chronically think and feel things like, *I won't be valued, regarded well, given a chance, accepted, understood.* Our ego and mind will trick us into thinking that what we can do won't matter, which eventually evolves into us thinking *we* don't matter. Remember, whatever it is we think, feel, or believe, God, the energy of the universe, our ego, and our soul always have the same answer for us: *You're right! Let me show you more!* In time, that will leave us feeling emotionally and physically exhausted, cynical, and powerless. Eventually what sets in is self-doubt, overwhelm, diminished engagement, job burnout, and even further into the process, depression. It's a slippery slope leading to *life* burnout.

In my career as an employee relations specialist I would often hear employees defending themselves when they were under review for poor job performance with "I was doing what I was told to do." Sometimes, they would elaborate that they knew it was never the direction that was going to get the results they were on the hook for. I would ask them, "Then why did you do it that way? Why wouldn't you share your ideas about what would get the desired results?"

I could predict the answer. It was always a variation of the same one: "Because that's what I was told to do, and it's useless to push back. No one listens anyway. They just want things done their way."

I would explore with the employee two scenarios connected with believing they could be fired for poor job performance. One, whether they would prefer being fired for executing someone else's idea that they never thought had a chance of being successful anyway? Or two, would they prefer being fired for offering their own idea that they thought might enable success?

Sometimes they would ask, "What does it matter, if I am going to be fired anyway?" I would say because in the one scenario where you offered a different option you did your best and even though it didn't work out, you can recover from the setback because you've kept your power. In the original scenario, you unwittingly yet willfully walked into failure, allowing the security of a job or someone else's favor to take away your power. That is much harder to recover from. Even if what you offer doesn't pay off, you can recover from doing what you thought was best. It's when we do what others tell us to do, believe it won't work, keep quiet, and it fails, that it becomes hard to recover.

Let's Get to Work ...

Purpose, personal power, and peace are possible from offering your work. They don't show up from your compliance, from results, from *doing the job*, from other people's power, from what others think of you, nor from a stamina for forcing yourself to show up and perform despite a blurred or depleted sense of self.

Often we think of our job and our work as one and the same. Or we think of our work as the place where we perform our job. However, there is a difference between doing your job and offering your work.

Your work is what you enable (versus do) for others and, therefore, align yourself with. It comes from within—it appeals to and evokes the power of the soul. A job on the other hand is how you make your living. It comes from something material, earthly, and outside yourself, like a business. It appeals to and evokes the power of the ego. Your work provides an opportunity for you to be a part of something bigger than just yourself. Whether that's an ability to serve a cause that matters to you, to provide for your family, or to enable yourself to affiliate with a community of people you care about learning from and offering your knowledge, skills, and talents to. A job enables you to experience being assigned a slice of responsibility that is a part of a larger organization. That slice of responsibility is defined by tasks that merely provide the typical opportunities in which your work, skills, and ability to impact others would be most valued on a regular basis. Our work and our skills stay with us as they are transferrable across many different jobs.

Unlike a job, our *work* defines us. It is that which we can't stop offering, no matter what happens in our life. *Your work* is offering and doing what no one else who was in that job could bring to it—not in the way you could. Understanding your intention and performing tasks through that intention (holding that intention in your mind, body, and soul while you perform the tasks associated with a job) *is* doing *your work*. Those who only complete tasks and meet goals within the assigned responsibilities of their job without awareness of the intention they have for others aren't doing *their work*. They probably aren't doing the job as well as they think they are either, especially if they only know an intention they have for themselves (i.e., promotion, bigger bonus, or favor with select individuals). What we accomplish by or for ourselves is never more meaningful than what we enable for others through our work.

Doing your job means doing the tasks that make up your job description in exchange for money and recognition. What follows is a sense that others hold the power to value, reward, and evolve us in our career. At best what follows is an ability to pay bills, an ability to detach from others who annoy us at times, and fleeting moments of escapism that occur to us as fulfillment.

Doing your work means doing the work you were put on this planet to do for others through an employer or a business of your own. You do this in exchange for a sense that you have power to make a meaningful difference and evolve the consciousness of yourself and others simultaneously. What follows is a sustained sense of fulfillment, relatedness, connection with others, ease in identifying opportunities to progress in your career and life, and operating with certainty that your next level of potential will be evident in time. A byproduct of that is an effortless flow of money, recognition, and other material rewards that will actually enhance your life versus destroy it and leave you feeling like no matter how much you get, it's never enough.

> Doing your work means doing the work you were put on this planet to do for others through an employer or a business of your own.

Doing your work is creating something. It's thrilling because it's adventurous, brave, and validating. *Devotion to your work* leads to knowing that how you impact others is how you too become impacted. *Doing your job* is performing within what is defined, expected, and justified. *Dedication to a job* often leads to a focus on how things impact only you.

Here are five examples of what you might be focused on if you are *dedicated to a job* versus *devoted to your work*:

1. tasks

2. how others seem to react to you and your contributions and wondering what that means for you (especially materially)

3. covering your ass (your reputation)

4. wondering why others don't value you as much as you think they should

5. getting out of work on time and as often as you can (e.g., vacations, leaving "on time," feeling a "need" to get out for lunch or breaks).

Doing your job, even if you like it, will never sustain your greatest sense of fulfillment on its own. Nor will it enable sustainable engagement or the most rewards you can ever achieve in your career. If you relate to any of the examples of doing a job, is there any wonder you may be feeling stuck, overwhelmed, less than engaged, or burned out at your job?

Being focused on *your job* is being focused on building and preserving your reputation. Your reputation is tied to your *past* performance. Being focused on "your work" is being focused on discovering and expanding your character. Your character exists in the present—IT IS your *presence*.

Which business have you been in?

A connection to a sense of purpose from serving others is among the most important things we are here to experience. It is necessary for the growth, development, and lasting elevation of our consciousness. Material rewards like promotions, pay increases, vacations, or distractions such as alcohol, drugs, video games, shopping, only numb a depleted ego temporarily. Remove the condition and there we are pining to feel a higher energy outside ourself to give us a (false) sense of personal power.

Granted, some jobs are a better match than others with your work. Yet experiencing satisfaction and fulfillment from *devotion to your work* has nothing to do with your job. You can do *your work* IN ANY JOB you have or will have in the future. The magnitude to which you get to discover, do, and be valued for *your work* is in your control. It starts with learning how to nurture yourself when you are thinking, feeling, or having an urge to behave in a way that is contrary to building your energy, being civil, or maintaining your sense of personal power.

Don't ever make a *job* more important than your *work*. Jobs are replaceable—you can always get another job. All your jobs make up your career. Your career is the story of years of service from *you doing your work in all the jobs* you have had to date. Your work never really "changes" as much as it evolves. *Your career* is the story of *your work* becoming clearer, expanding, and evolving to make a difference for others in this world. What validates who you are and brings fulfillment is *devotion to your work* in any and all jobs you have and will have. You do this, of course, while giving yourself nurturing care as you face the challenges that come with all jobs. Embrace your job experiences good and bad. Jobs are like tours you take on a journey of self-discovery, growth, and evolution. The souvenir of engagement at each job is a more expanded sense of self-actualization.

> Your career is the story of your work becoming clearer, expanding, and evolving to make a difference for others in this world.

Offering what you have to offer time and time again without regard for whether or not it's deserved or will be socially acceptable is the truth you must accept and surrender to in order to feel connected to a sustainable sense of power and to open up a connection with a sense of purpose.

I talked with my client who wanted to be on a "winning team," and discovered that the truth was that having early "winning team" experiences in his career enabled him to learn what winning teams looked like to him (Step 1—Observe).

He realized that at this point in his career, just being on a winning team was no longer enough for him to feel fulfilled. He felt blocked in what was once an easy ability to align himself with winning teams because he had evolved into an eagle who was ready to fly the coop from such experiences (Step 2—Pause—be with that feeling).

He was ready to further develop and apply his skills around creating such teams. I suggested he trust himself to figure out how to nurture himself through the journey of creating winning teams on this planet (Step 3—Engage). He adjusted his standard for performance by no longer complaining about team dysfunction.

Instead he would step up and offer his personality, talents, knowledge, skills, abilities, experience, personal and professional boundaries, and *service*, to others. He was ready to enable a possibility he could see as being "winning." He figured out that he could give himself support to do so by learning more and more about "winning teams" and offering his unique vision of that to others with every interaction. This is Step 4—Nurture! He could see that such a shift in his mindset and actions would enable him to feel supported as a professional who was now ready to align with and be accountable for creating or enabling winning teams and develop them within organizations that were not winning.

He applied a soul-fulfilling strategy to his approach to work, OPENed his ability to be engaged at his job, and got back on the path of purpose.

And Be OPEN

If you feel that your current job is a mismatch, accept that in order to be aligned with work you love, nobody needs to make it safe for you to offer what you have to offer. In addition, you don't have to believe that anyone deserves what you have to offer. You must surrender to the journey of discovering your sense of purpose. You *OPEN* your ability to surrender to that journey by first learning how to take care of yourself when faced with dark or challenging circumstances so that you don't fall victim to feelings of exhaustion, cynicism, or powerlessness.

I believe the key to feeling better rested, more civil, and more powerful is to be fully present to a sense of clarity, confidence, and conviction for your work. The same can be achieved in reverse. You can enable clarity, confidence, and conviction for your work by practicing strategies that boost your ability to be more energized, more civil, and more powerful.

> I believe the key to feeling better rested, more civil, and more powerful is to be fully present to a sense of clarity, confidence, and conviction for your work. The same can be achieved in reverse. You can enable clarity, confidence, and conviction for your work by practicing strategies that boost your ability to be more energized, more civil, and more powerful.

Nature is always balancing itself. So if you are here on this planet, you are here because you are part of what keeps the planet's energy in balance: collective egos and souls functioning in balance together. Thankfully, the universe is patient and it gives you time to figure out how to discover and balance your individual ego and soul. The universe is also a teacher full of clever ways to get you to learn and apply yourself in the world. It's always offering you hints on how to move your ego to the passenger seat so that you can more easily know and open your soul.

The OPEN Method shows you how to open up to your thoughts, urges, and feelings, and how to respond to them by caring for yourself in ways that awaken your soul. An awakened soul will naturally offset wounded, ego-fueled reactions that only keep you stuck, confused, exhausted, cynical, powerless, less than engaged, or burned out.

All you need right now to align your energy with the path of purpose is to always remember to practice the OPEN Method. At first, you will be slow in your ability to recognize opportunities to practice the method. I suggest you accommodate yourself as a beginning practitioner. To accommodate yourself, simply write "OPEN" on several sticky notes and place them in key places to remind you to practice the method. Take a picture of one of your sticky notes and make it your screen saver on your phone. Practice is the best way to learn, experience, and prepare yourself to receive and handle a connection with a sense of purpose and calling for your work—and your life.

Gnothi Seauton is inscribed at the Temple of Apollo at Delphi. It means "know thyself." Knowing yourself is your greatest opportunity to make a meaningful difference in the world. Knowing yourself primarily means knowing your ego and your soul and having an awareness of when self-nurturing is required to keep them working in harmony. To know your soul and ego has nothing to do with judging them—instead, seek to OPEN them. In OPENing them, we detach from connections that put the ego in charge, such as connections to *a job*. Instead, we enable ourselves to connect with what puts our soul in charge (which nurtures and enables both the soul and the ego to work together purposefully), such as connections to *our work*. In doing so, we evolve naturally to be at peace with ourselves, others, and this world. When we *OPEN* ourselves to purpose and peace within, we notice opportunities to reflect the possibility of purpose and peace to others. In return, we notice purpose and peace in the world around us.

ACKNOWLEDGMENTS

Writing this book has been one of the most supportive experiences of my life. It has been a work in the making for nearly thirty years. The book started to exist once I started working in Human Resources. Of course at that time I had no idea a book was growing within me.

In a down economy, I was just so grateful to have landed an internship at a prestigious financial services firm. I will always be grateful to Walter Kehoe, Caroline Sieber, and Eileen Armstrong, for offering me not just my first "real job" but also offering me the opportunity to learn, make mistakes, mature, grow, and at times take some running-on-instinct risks to serve some of the smartest and most respectful professionals I have ever had the pleasure to work with in my career.

I'd also like to thank Linda Curran, Lewis Sandy, MD, Sandra Collins, Kathy McCarthy, and Joe Braunstein for offering me professional opportunities that further expanded my knowledge and leadership while enabling me to clarify and honor my values. I am forever a better person for having grown up professionally under their strong and competent wings.

Along the way I have had the honor of working and serving with some of the most amazing people. Mary Jo Schmitt, Lara Gartenberg, Regina McGough, Jinny Jun, Belinda Jones, David Waldman, Evan LaHuta, Anthony Pratofiorito, Ninfa Vasquez, Brian Justice, Bianka

Douglas, Bob Nelson, Jennifer Rafford, Sue Chegwidden, Rachel Grace, Denise Cliatt, Linda Bodnar, Leslie D'Ascoli, and Romi Boucher, I wouldn't have learned or laughed as much as I did over my corporate years without each of you. You made every day a day I wanted to come to work—no matter what.

I'd also like to thank the amazing team of colleagues I worked alongside when I was head of Human Resources: Mary Kelly, Mary Powers, Jacque Weiss, Noreen MacMahon, Steven Gibson, Sam Gaines, Marilyn Herbert, John Finnan, Tennille Rudolph, Liliana Merizaldi, and Felicia Garland. The support, collaboration, and care from you and your teams enabled me to feel strong and courageous through all the personal and professional highs and lows at that time in my life. I am so grateful to have stepped up with each of you as we all expanded in so many ways personally and professionally. Each of you, and my time with you, will always be special to me. A special thank you to Jacque for teaching me to "always assume best intentions."

Transitioning from corporate to my own business enabled me to evolve in so many ways. I think it would be nearly impossible to list everyone who has left an indelible impression on inspiring my business, my message, my coaching and training programs, this book, and certainly on me as a person! No doubt the most important people are all the employees, managers, executives, and corporate and private clients who have taught me what matters most to people when they are feeling depleted, stuck, and confused. Through your pain and sharing relatedness with it, I have discovered universal patterns in how people become depleted, stuck, and confused, and how and why they stay that way, and what can help them move through such experiences.

I'm also grateful for all the employees, managers, executives, and corporate and private clients who have shown me what people who contribute with a sense of purpose and are happy and fulfilled have in common. Through applying what I observed in you into my work and life, I was able to achieve a sense of purpose and fulfillment beyond what I ever would have thought was possible. In addition to all of you, there have been other personal and professional people who deserve thanks for enabling me to bring what I achieved for myself into the world in a broader sense.

To start, thank you to my mastermind geniuses—Dana Lee, Debbie Lonergan, Ellen Rogin, Maggie Dillon-Katz, Annette Naif, and Jodi Graber. We've come a long way from leaving our academic and corporate backgrounds to starting our businesses and coaching practices. Our meet-ups have always been therapeutic, enlightening, and fun! Ellen and Maggie, I am so glad I met you in San Diego and so grateful we still connect regularly after ten years. I love our authentic exchanges and soul-felt discussions. Thank you for being a part of this journey.

I also especially want to thank some dear friends. Dana, I am so grateful I hunted you down in Los Angeles at a networking event and I am even more grateful you were open and willing to connect weekly with a fellow assertive Jersey gal. It's been over ten years that we have been meeting weekly to talk shop, cry through the tough times, share tips and tools, and build a lasting friendship. I love you, Dana! Debbie, I am so grateful you ignored all the schoolwork I would try to get through while hiding at a remote table waiting for my waitressing shift to start back when we were in college. Having you as my friend over the past thirty plus years has been one of the greatest gifts in my life; having your support in growing my business has been even sweeter. I will love and cherish you forever! Also, thank you to Karen for teaching me to "cocoon" and Ciara for the experiences you shared with me from the practices offered in this book.

A special thanks to the smart and experienced professionals I have learned from about how to establish my business, my message, and my presence in a community. Wendy Y. Bailey, Beth Lefevre, Ulrike Berzau, Doria Gambino, Derrick Sweet, Melody Godfred, Rebeccca Henninger, Angela Kubisky, Joe Nazzaro and Laura Cust. You each made what was daunting to me at times so clear and so much easier.

Along with everyone I just mentioned, a huge thank you also goes to those who were most pivotal in this book coming to life. Janice Gregory—thank you so much for sharing your degree in English from Harvard University with me. With a degree from Harvard or not, you are amazingly gifted and without meeting you I never would have gotten the final boost I needed to sit down and get this book *done*! Your feedback has been absolutely instrumental in turning what I thought I had in me to something so much more. Ellen, Maggie, Bob, and Dana—thank you as well for your valuable feedback. In the five of you I feel like I have a beta-reader *dream team*!

Janet Bray Attwood, Chris Attwood, Marci Shimoff, Geoff Affleck, Nina Shoroplova, Lisa Turner, Dr. George Lucey, and Shawn Achor. Your mentorship, help, support, and shoulders that I stand on related to this book and getting my message out there in general has been incredible. I am in awe of your level of generosity, encouragement, and inspiration.

Lastly, big hugs, love and gratitude go to my husband, Bob, my children, Michael and Grace, their cousins and caregivers, Allison and Courtney. Grace, if it wasn't for you coming into our lives, none of this work would have ever been shared with the world. I am so blessed to have all of you in my life. I couldn't ask for a better husband or kids!

And a very final thank you to my two dogs Lucy and Roxie, who kept me company so many lonely days on end while I was creating my business and writing this book.

All of you have inspired me to find *my work*, share my experiences, perspective, and authentic self to (hopefully) make a meaningful difference for those who feel amotivated, stuck, overwhelmed, tired, cynical, powerless, and burned out. I am grateful for all the relationships mentioned and unmentioned here for offering me greater clarity of what love, support, inspiration, and purpose look like for me.

RESOURCES

Courses

Landmark Education

Mindset Mentorship by Dana Lee

Nonviolent Communication

Sedona Soul Adventures

The Work of Byron Katie

Books and Articles

Achor, Shawn. *Before Happiness: The 5 Hidden Keys to Achieving Success, Spreading Happiness, and Sustaining Positive Change.* New York, NY: Random House Audio, 2013.

——. *The Happiness Advantage: How a Positive Brain Fuels Success in Work and Life.* New York, NY: Random House Audio, 2010.

Brady, Joan. *God on a Harley: A Spiritual Fable.* New York, NY: Pocket Books, 1996.

Bray Attwood, Janet, and Chris Attwood. *The Passion Test: The Effortless Path to Discovering Your Life Purpose.* New York, NY: Plume, 2008.

Coelho, Paulo. *The Alchemist*. New York, NY: Harper One, 1993.

David, Susan, PhD. *Emotional Agility: Get Unstuck, Embrace Change, and Thrive in Work and Life*. New York, NY: Penguin Audio, 2016.

Dennett, Carrie. "Could walking barefoot on grass improve your health? Some research suggests it can." The *Washington Post*, July 10, 2018.

Feintzeig, Rachel. "Feeling Burned Out at Work? Join the Club." The *Wall Street Journal*, February 28, 2017.

Frankl, Viktor E. *Man's Search for Meaning*. Ashland, OR: Blackstone Audio, Inc., 2004.

Harrell, Keith. *Attitude Is Everything: 10 Life-Changing Steps to Turning Attitude into Action*. New York, NY: Harper Collins Publishers, Inc. 2005.

Hawkins, David R, MD, PhD. *Letting Go: The Pathway of Surrender*. Carlsbad, CA: Hay House, 2012.

———. *Power vs. Force: The Hidden Determinants of Human Behavior*. Carlsbad, CA: Hay House, 2012.

Hay, Louise L. *You Can Heal Your Life*. Santa Monica, CA: Hay House, 1987.

His Holiness the Dalai Lama and Howard C. Cutler, MD. *The Art of Happiness at Work*. New York, NY: Riverhead Books, 2003.

Katie, Byron with Stephen Mitchell. *Loving What Is: Four Questions that Can Change Your Life*. New York, NY: Random House Audio, 2016.

Leiter, Michael P., and Christina Maslach. *Banishing Burnout: Six Strategies for Improving Your Relationship with Work*. San Francisco, CA: Jossey-Bass, 2005.

Neff, Kristen, PhD. *Self-Compassion: The Proven Power of Being Kind to Yourself*. New York, NY: William Morrow, 2011.

Schucman, Helen, PhD, with William Thetford, PhD. *A Course in Miracles*. Novato, CA: Foundation for Inner Peace, 2007.

Shimoff, Marci with Carol Kline. *Happy for No Reason: 7 Steps to Being Happy from the Inside Out*. New York, NY: Free Press, 2008.

Other Resources

Achor, Shawn. www.shawnachor.com/

American Management Association. www.amanet.org

Breathwork at Global Professional Breathwork Alliance. breathwork-alliance.com

Brown, Brené. brenebrown.com

Campbell, Joseph. Works by Campbell: Books at www.jcf.org/works/by-campbell/books/

David, Susan, PhD. www.susandavid.com

Hawkins, David. veritaspub.com

Hay, Louise. www.louisehay.com

Heart-Focused Breathing at HeartMath Institute. www.heart-math.org/articles-of-the-heart/the-math-of-heartmath/heart-focused-breathing/

His Holiness the Dalai Lama. www.dalailama.com

Kid Snippets www.youtube.com/user/BoredShortsTV

The Maslach Burnout Inventory (MBI) and Areas of Worklife Survey (AWS) by Christina Maslach and Michael Leiter

Neff, Kristen, PhD. https://self-compassion.org

Passion Test. www.thepassiontest.com

Somatic Psychotherapy. usabp.org/Body-Psychotherapy-versus-Somatic-Psychology/

PERMISSIONS

Book epigraph printed from *The Art of Happiness at Work* by the Dalai Lama and Howard C. Cutler, MD. Riverhead Books, published by The Berkley Publishing Group, A division of Penguin Group (USA) Inc., 375 Hudson Street, New York, NY 10014. All rights reserved, used with permission from His Holiness, the Dalai Lama.

Excerpts reprinted from *Attitude Is Everything: 10 Life-changing Steps to Turning Attitude into Action* by Keith Harrell, HarperCollins Publishers, 195 Broadway, New York, NY 10007. All rights reserved, used with permission.

Excerpts reprinted from *Meditations to Heal Your Life,* copyright ©2000 by Louise Hay, Hay House, Inc., Carlsbad, CA. All rights reserved, used with permission.

All quotes from *A Course in Miracles,* copyright ©1992, 1999, 2007 by the Foundation for Inner Peace, 448 Ignacio Blvd., #306, Novato, CA 94949, www.acim.org and info@acim.org, used with permission.

Excerpts reprinted from *Success Is for You: Using Heart-Centered Power Principles for Lasting Abundance and Fulfillment* by David R.

AUTHOR BIO

Gina Calvano has lived the experience of transforming herself from being an accredited professional (who was burned out and painfully questioning her career choice) to being a happy and successful corporate head of a busy human resources department. Since then she has segued to being an independent career coach who helps people live their purpose and feel destined for success.

That journey showed her how to conquer burnout, understand the fear of job instability, and discover clarity, confidence, conviction, and love for her work—and life.

Throughout her corporate career, Gina has maintained a goal to work at organizations of various sizes that are going through significant business challenges. She did this to understand how global and functional business goals can be balanced with the personal and professional desires and challenges of employees at all levels of experience.

She designed, implemented, and led initiatives related to organizational design and development; policy development; employee relations and investigations; environmental scans; morale improvement;

performance management and improvement; rewards and recognition; executive coaching; recruiting, retaining, and developing talent; compensation; orientation; employment legal compliance; health and wellness; training; and HR systems.

Working with people of different backgrounds and levels of aspiration, from those who are just entering the workforce to those who have already achieved the highest levels in their careers, she believes in teaching each one that they are essential and critical to the overall success of their company, industry, and ultimately the world and its people.

After the birth of her second child, Gina was inspired to leave her cushy Vice President role as Head of Human Resources (even though she loved it dearly) and pivot to career coaching. She knew she had no desire to be "Super Woman" and the chance to experience being solely dedicated to her young family was never going to come around again in this lifetime. About four months after being home with her family, she decided to combine her talents and interests with her corporate achievements to create her coaching practice.

Today, Gina is dedicated to helping others learn how to gain clarity for their talents and to be connected to their purpose and calling to feel destined for success. She is certified as both a coach and a Senior Professional in Human Resources (SPHR), with over twenty years of experience as a human resources executive in both the private and non-profit sectors and over ten years of experience as a certified career coach. Gina created the Discover Your Life Calling Bootcamp™, a step-by-step process that enables people to discover their personal brand and values and match them to college majors, jobs, industries, and leisure pursuits.

Gina is also a contributing author to *Breakthrough!: Inspirational Strategies for an Audaciously Authentic Life.* She graduated from Seton Hall University and lives with her husband, two children, and two dogs in Morris County, NJ.

AUTHOR SERVICES

Gina has dedicated her career to helping individuals and companies that feel drained to discover and offer what they can be counted on for, no matter what. Through her work she combines her strategic corporate expertise and accreditations with transformational thinking tools, coaching, and strategies to enable conscious approaches to living and working. That enables her clients to experience feeling clarified, confident and convicted for their work and enjoy inevitable happiness and success. Gina does this by showing them how to do three things:

1. Get aligned with sustainable sources of fulfillment to recover from and prevent burnout

2. Connect to a sense of purpose and discover their true work— what they ultimately want to enable for others and be valued for in return

3. Become masterful at recognizing opportunities that are perfectly served by their talents and skills

In essence, she enables her clients to do powerful work they love despite being in a job they may hate, and to win favor over competitors, even over those who may have more experience.

Gina offers initial consultations to discuss challenges and even do an exercise to help gain insight into what a person's true work actually is.

Website: www.indigoforce.com

Email: info@indigoforce.com

NOTES

[1] Jae Yup Jung and John McCormick, "Occupational Decision-Related Processes for Amotivated Adolescents: Confirmation of a Model," *Sage Journals*, doi/10.1177/0894845310367638

[2] Annamarie Mann and Jim Harter, "The Worldwide Employee Engagement Crisis," *Gallup*. static1.squarespace.com/static/552b3ee0e4b016252ff74ac0/t/59b652928dd04187 fcfd085a/1505120914868/The+Worldwide+Employee+Engagement+Crisis+Gallup.pdf

[3] Ben Wigert, Sangeeta Agrawal, Kristin Barry and Ellyn Maesea, "The Wellbeing-Engagement Paradox of 2020," *Gallup*. www.gallup.com/workplace/336941/wellbeing-engagement-paradox-2020.aspx

[4] Social Psychology Network, entry for Christina Maslach, https://maslach.socialpsychology.org/publications

[5] World Health Organization, "Burn-out an 'occupational phenomenon': International Classification of Diseases." www.who.int/news/item/28-05-2019-burn-out-an-occupational-phenomenon-international-classification-of-diseases

[6] Michael P. Leiter and Christina Maslach, Science Direct, *Burnout Research*, Volume 3, Issue 4, December 2016, pages 89-100, "Latent burnout profiles: A new approach to understanding the burnout experience." doi.org/10.1016/j.burn.2016.09.001

[7] Christina Maslach and Michael P. Leiter, chapter 24 in *HBR Guide to Beating Burnout* by Harvard Business Review Press, 2020

[8] Leiter and Maslach, "Latent burnout profiles"

[9] Laurie Fickman, "Job Interest Not a Big Predictor of Job Satisfaction" in University of Houston, News and Events, November 11, 2020, https://uh.edu/news-events/stories/2020/november-2020/11112020-kevin-hoff-interest-job-satisfaction.php

[10] Christina Maslach, Susan E. Jackson, Michael P. Leiter, Wilmar B. Schaufeli, and Richard L. Schwab, "Maslach Burnout Toolkit"™, www.mindgarden.com/184-maslach-burnout-toolkit | Michael P. Leiter and Christina Maslach, "Areas of Worklife Survey." www.mindgarden.com/274-areas-of-worklife-survey

[11] Rachel Feintzeig, "Feeling Burned Out at Work? Join the Club," The Wall Street Journal. www.wsj.com/articles/feeling-burned-out-at-work-join-the-club-1488286801

[12] Jim Harter, "U.S. Employee Engagement Rises Following Wild 2020," Gallup Workplace. www.gallup.com/workplace/330017/employee-engagement-rises-following-wild-2020.aspx

[13] Karen Brans and Philippe Verduyn, "Intensity and Duration of Negative Emotions: Comparing the Role of Appraisals and Regulation Strategies," March 26, 2014, doi. org/10.1371/journal.pone.0092410

[14] Carrie Dennett, "Could walking barefoot on grass improve your health? Some research suggests it can.," The Washington Post. www.washingtonpost.com/lifestyle/wellness/could-walking-barefoot-on-the-grass-improve-your-health-the-science-behind-grounding/2018/07/05/12de5d64-7be2-11e8-aeee-4d04c8ac6158_story.html

[15] Leiter and Maslach, "Latent burnout profiles"

[16] Luke 5:17

[17] Baylor University, "Cynical Hostility Presents Potential Pathway to Cardiovascular Disease, Study Finds," www.baylor.edu/mediacommunications/news.php?action=story&story=221031

[18] Leiter and Maslach, "Latent burnout profiles"

[19] Reham Al Taher, MSc, "The 5 Founding Fathers and A History of Positive Psychology," July 5, 2020, in PositivePsychology.com at https://positivepsychology.com/founding-fathers/

[20] Kelly Miller, "Is Happiness Genetic and What Causes It?" December 10, 2020, in PositivePsychology.com at https://positivepsychology.com/is-happiness-genetic/

[21] Marci Shimoff, Happy for No Reason: 7 Steps to Being Happy from the Inside Out, introduction, p. 6

[22] Ronald E. Riggio, PhD, "The 4 Styles of Humor," April 15, 2015, Psychology Today at www.psychologytoday.com/us/blog/cutting-edge-leadership/201504/the-4-styles-humor

[23] Elaine Houston, BSc, "The Importance of Positive Relationships in the Workplace," April 14, 2021, PositivePsychology.com at https://positivepsychology.com/positive-relationships-workplace/

[24] Leiter and Maslach, "Latent burnout profiles"

Made in the USA
Las Vegas, NV
19 May 2022

49104330R00163